Let's Write

by Nancy Areglado
and Mary Dill

SCHOLASTIC
PROFESSIONAL BOOKS

New York • Toronto • London • Auckland • Sydney

Cover design by Laurel Marx
Cover photograph by Andrew Levine
Interior design by Lauren Leon

ISBN 0-590-93102-4

Acknowledgments

To Roscoe Mack, who knows everything there is to know about computers.

To the students at Rolling Valley School, whose writing never ceases to amaze us!

To the students' parents for their cooperation.

To our super Rolling Valley staff for their dedication to teaching.

To all of our friends and relatives for their kind words of encouragement.

Last, and by no means least, to our families, who have truly been our cheerleaders—Kristin, Kimberly, and Julie Areglado; Stephanie Dill; and Sybil and P.J. Dunegan.

Meet the Authors & Contributors

Nancy Areglado is a reading specialist and Reading Recovery teacher at Rolling Valley Elementary School in Fairfax County, Virginia. She also coordinates the schoolwide portfolio assessment and language arts programs at Rolling Valley. Nancy received national certification as an Early Childhood Generalist from the National Board for Professional Teachers. Currently, she is a finalist for *The Washington Post* Agnes Meler Award as the 1997 Fairfax County Public School Teacher of the Year. She is an independent language arts consultant and presents locally and nationally at conferences as well as for school systems, universities, and colleges. Nancy has taught kindergarten through grade eight and worked with kindergarten-primary staff in two school systems in Massachusetts as an early-childhood consultant and a language arts coordinator. While residing in Massachusetts, she served as co-organizer and past president of a large teacher's association in the Berkshire region and received the International Reading Association's "Celebrate Literacy Award" from the Berkshire Reading Council. She is a co-author of *Portfolios in the Classroom—A Teacher's Sourcebook* (Scholastic Professional Books, 1993) and has published many articles in educational journals.

Mary Dill is principal of Rolling Valley Elementary, a K-6 school in Fairfax County, Virginia, where she implemented the integrated language arts philosophy throughout the school. The school received the International Reading Association's Exemplary Reading Award in 1992 and is the first school in the state of Virginia to receive this award. Mary Dill was nominated by the P.T.A. and teachers for the Fairfax County Administrator of the Year. Mary's professional career includes primary teacher, resource teacher, coordinator of the gifted-and-talented program, and human-relations specialist. She is a co-author of *Portfolios in the Classroom—A Teacher's Sourcebook* and has written several articles on language arts in educational journals. She is a frequent presenter on writing as well as all aspects of language arts and portfolio assessment locally and nationally.

Kathy Godwin has taught kindergarten at Rolling Valley Elementary School in Fairfax County, Virginia for eight years. She received her BA in Early Childhood Education from the University of South Carolina. Kathy is an independent language arts consultant and has presented workshops at local and state conferences. Recently, she was involved in an English as a Second Language (ESL) collaboration project for the Fairfax County Public Schools.

Lisa Holm is a first grade teacher at Rolling Valley Elementary School in Fairfax County, Virginia. She received her master's degree in Special Education from George Mason University and has worked with students in grades kindergarten through seven. Lisa is an independent language arts consultant and has presented workshops at local, state, and national conferences. In 1997, she received national certification as an Early Childhood Generalist from the National Board of Professional Teaching Standards.

Melissa Miller is a graduate of California University of Pennsylvania with a BS in Elementary/Early Childhood Education. She has taught preschool and kindergarten. Currently, she is entering her third year as a second grade teacher at Rolling Valley Elementary School in Springfield, Virginia. Melissa has presented workshops on the writing process.

Introduction

Let's Write grew out of our efforts to understand how kindergarten, first-, and second-grade students become proficient, enthusiastic writers. It was also inspired by our fellow teachers, who wanted a variety of ideas, lessons, writing strategies, and management techniques to reignite the spark in their writing workshops. They knew they needed to instill new energy in their lessons and practices, and to find ways to make writing workshop easier to manage. They wanted to hear their students cheer instead of groan when they announced it was time for writing.

Every lesson in this book was developed from an actual classroom need, and has been field-tested with teachers across the country. Again and again, the teachers we met told us they need the nuts and bolts of how to implement an exciting writing program that turns kids on to writing. They asked for a how-to book. We hope and trust that *Let's Write* answers this need.

—Nancy Areglado and Mary Dill

Table of Contents

Foreward

- ❖ "How can I help children get started on their writing?"
- ❖ "What are some organizational tips for successfully managing my writing program?"
- ❖ "How can I assess what children have learned in writing during the last few months?"

Let's Write is an excellent resource for helping teachers find answers to these, and other, questions about writing in the primary grades. The book is written for both beginning and experienced teachers—all those who search for ways to encourage children's growth as writers, and who are concerned about developing successful writers' workshops in their classrooms.

The authors of the book—Nancy Areglado, a reading specialist, and Mary Dill, a school principal, both at Rolling Valley Elementary School, in Fairfax County, Virginia—have written from personal experience. Working in a school with a diverse student population, the authors address a wide variety of issues, all of which they encounter in their own working day. The strategies—from how to encourage the hesitant writer to how to celebrate children's accomplishments—have met with much enthusiasm by teachers and students in Rolling Valley Elementary, and in classes around the country.

Support for Writers' Workshop

I believe that a rich, well-organized writers' workshop is important to the success of children's growth as writers. To create an effective program, teachers need to be adept in many areas: They must understand the elements of writing and be able to set up daily routines; they must be skilled in how to model writing strategies for the whole class, for small groups, and for individuals; and they must be able to hold effective teacher/student conferences, drawing on a wide repertoire of strategies—from "sharing the pen" to creating criteria charts for writing—to facilitate children's early writing attempts.

Fortunately, *Let's Write* addresses all these issues. Building from a description of the developmental levels of writing—from scribbling to standard writing—the book goes on to detail a variety of ways to support children as they move from planning to publishing a piece. In addition, this well-organized resource provides a wealth of other specific strategies that help children revise their work. It even includes a special chapter on integrating writing through social studies, science, and mathematics.

Teaching Tips

Throughout the book, three teachers from Rolling Valley—Kathy Godwin (kindergarten), Lisa Holm (first grade), and Melissa Miller (second grade)—share vignettes about writing sessions in their classrooms, a time when children learn from one another and from the teacher. The anecdotes are particularly lively and provide concrete details that support points made by the authors. For example, the chapter on helping children plan a piece is augmented by practical tips from Kathy Godwin on using "I Can Write About It" planning sheets.

Let's Write makes me want to return to kindergarten, first-grade, and second-grade classrooms to try out the ideas and strategies I've learned. Fortunately, this book is by teachers and for teachers, and provides answers to our basic questions about teaching young children to write.

I expect it will be a treasured addition to your professional library. It certainly is to mine.

—*Bobbi Fisher*

Chapter One

The Teacher's Role in Developing Writers

"Are you going to read a book to me tonight?" begged Mary Dill's grandson, P.J. "You know, my favorite one—*Leo the Late Bloomer.*"

After hearing the "lion book" many times, three-year-old P.J. could anticipate what was coming next on each page. In fact, he invented a story similar to the "lion book," as he experimented with telling stories. For P.J., reading was a vehicle that led him to create tales aloud, which also prompted him to put on paper a story that he could read back to his grandmother. As with all developing writers, P.J. had made an important connection—he learned that print represents meaning.

As soon as children learn to talk, they convey ideas enthusiastically. Renee Fuller, a noted psychologist, defines this as "storying," a child's ability to create wholeness—in the form of stories—out of one's experiences. According to Fuller, storying occurs at the most formative stage of intellectual development. P.J.'s fascination with stories he has heard played a significant role in his desire to grasp a pencil with his stubby fingers and make scribble marks on paper. P.J., like other children, writes stories to accompany books that are read to him, and creates new stories based on his experiences, his fantasies, and his interactions with others. Interestingly, no matter what the culture, children pass through a developmental stage in which they are compelled by an inner desire to communicate their thoughts through writing. It's rare that beginning writers say, "I don't know how to write."

Children come to school with an innate curiosity about writing. Many scribble and experiment on paper with print-like letters. Since research shows that young children feel they *can* write, what is our role in providing a supportive environment that makes them *want* to write? We need to provide an environment in which the social and physical conditions promote writing.

Social Conditions *that* Promote Writing

Children thrive at Rolling Valley Elementary, where writing is valued. Our young students are part of a community of writers, where all efforts are appreciated and approximations rewarded. We continually develop an atmosphere of trust, so that students are willing to take the risk of sharing their thinking and their written work.

Puneet and Kelly eagerly share the projects they made and the predictions they wrote about fairy tales. Writing predictions helps students think about events for their own stories.

❖ **Write with the children.** To develop a trusting relationship, we write with the children and share our own writing with them. In this collaborative environment, students learn from one another as well as from the teacher, and the teacher learns from the students.

❖ **Surround students with print.** The written word awakens children's longing to write. When children are surrounded by signs, charts, stories, and poems, they see that writing has a purpose, that print conveys meaning. They notice words, phrases, and sentences, and begin to use words and phrases they see around them in their own writing. Educator Brian Cambourne refers to this process as immersion in a print-rich environment, in which children are shown how print works.

❖ **Show children's writing.** Displaying their work assures children that writing is important, and that their role as writers is respected by others. Donald Graves has said that children write "to have an exchange of meaning"; showing student work supports this natural urge to communicate something about ourselves to others.

Jayme uses the class-generated contraction chart to fix her spelling of *don't*. Often, students use words from charts, Words Walls, and other students' work in their writing.

Brett types his poem for publication. Publishing with the computer motivates students to take pieces to final copy.

❖ **Involve students in writing.** Students need to be creatively involved with writing experiences. They need to experience the writing process first-hand, to practice it with the teacher, so they can then apply that knowledge on their own. Frank Smith calls this process *engagement*.

❖ **Make writing centers accessible.** To have students use the writing center daily, clearly label the materials and make sure they are within children's reach. Some teachers in our school separate the tools into two centers: one for writing, the other for publishing.

In Melissa Miller's second-grade writing center, students can easily locate all writing materials.

Kindergartners Brian and Brook read their journals to each other. Designating places in your classroom where children can share ideas promotes the social aspect of writing.

❖**Encourage discussion.** Students need to be able to listen to one another read aloud their writing, and discuss ideas. They need to be able to concentrate on what classmates say about their work. And so the physical arrangement of the room—specifically, students' desks or tables—is an important way to promote children's writerliness. Regie Routman encourages teachers to team up with a colleague to model a discussion, so children learn how to listen well to one another.

❖ **Set aside daily writing time.** In our classrooms, students write each day during regularly scheduled blocks of time. We make sure children are aware of their own daily writing plan. With a predictable writing time, they can plan what they will write that day.

❖ **Give choice in writing topics.** If writing is to be joyous and not drudgery, students need to have a choice in what they write about. Although we teach our students to write for different purposes and across the curriculum, we always, in each lesson, give a degree of topic choice.

Brad worked for several sessions during the writers' workshop to complete his dinosaur project. Writing every day made the project flow smoothly.

❖ **Model writing strategies.** When our students see us write, they want to write. They see the value of the skill. Donald Graves has said that "being a writer yourself is perhaps the most important thing you can do to help children learn to write." We model writing in a number of different ways:

1. Compose think-alouds. We think aloud and compose writing in front of the students. For example, using a large piece of chart paper, we show students how we create a story lead. We "think aloud" several possible leads, then we select the one that will grab the reader's attention. We demonstrate this strategy repeatedly, so students will understand the process we are showing. Neglecting this vital step—and just showing a final piece—leaves students in the dark, wondering what steps led to the finished, "seamless" product.

2. Create mock samples. To show a particular skill—such as staying on-topic—we create two samples of writing (one strong, the other weak), then use those to help children see the differences. We also use the samples to develop with children criteria charts that describe the elements of good writing.

3. Use real literature. We use literature to illustrate the craft of writing. For example, we read aloud *The Little Mouse, The Red Ripe Strawberries, and The Big, Hungry Bear*, by Don and Audrey Wood, to show that vivid words make a piece of writing come alive.

4. Invite student participation. We involve students in the modeling. For example, if our lesson is on how to use a picture graphic organizer to select topics, we invite several students to assist by coloring pictures of ideas for topics in sections on the organizer.

5. Share your work. We share our own pieces of writing, from first drafts to final copies.

Nancy Areglado models a focus lesson on writing endings. Showing children how we make decisions as writers helps them learn the writing process.

We use the pieces to point out writing skills, and often contrast them with other versions of what we've written, which often lack focus, or rich details, or compelling leads and endings.

6. Use good work by students. Often, we model writing strategies using samples of students' work. We always get the student's permission beforehand, and we only point out the positive aspects of the piece. We never use a child's piece of writing to demonstrate an area that needs improvement.

❖ **Integrate writing throughout the curriculum.** We integrate writing across the curriculum (such as in math or social studies), so that children can better formulate ideas and make connections in those subject areas. We also put their published writing on display. What's more, visitors to the room can tell at a glance which themes the students have been studying, such as the seasons and tall-tale heroes.

❖ **Publish students' writing.** Perhaps the most important step we can take to support our students as writers is to publish their writing. Publishing celebrations such as Authors' Day—when students' families are invited to honor student writers in the classroom—send a message to the children that what they have to say is valued. Compiling stories into books that circulate through a lending library is another good way to give children the thrill of authorship.

An example of published flip books about Spring. Flip books are a quick and easy publishing technique.

Second-grade students publish poetry about Paul Bunyan. Inviting children to write historically based poems is an effective way to incorporate social studies and language arts.

Physical Conditions *that* Promote Writing

We want our classrooms to hum with the voices of writers editing together, reading drafts aloud, publishing pieces, and proudly announcing their literary debuts, like Joshua did when he said, "Have I got a story for you!" as he waved his book in the air. We want to hear conversations like the one that follows, for they signal to us that both the social climate and the physical setup of the classroom promote the joy of writing:

Joanna: Joel, are you taking my whale book home again today to read?
Joel: I love whales. That's what your book is about!
Joanna: Gee, thanks! I'm writing another good book now about how whales have babies.

How do you create this buzz of excitement? Organizing an inviting and physically defined writing center is key to making writing an integral, welcome part of a young child's life.

ORGANIZING A WRITERS' WORKSHOP IN KINDERGARTEN

The first thing you'll want to do is set up writing centers. Begin by assessing the developmental needs of students. Are they ready to rotate to writing centers during the writers' workshop, or should the centers move to the students? Kindergarten teacher Kathy Godwin uses three types of writing centers. One is stationary, and two are centers for conferring and publishing that are portable. Her students move to the stationary writing center during center time, but during writers' workshop, the portable publishing center caddies, stocked with supplies for editing and publishing, move to the students.

❖ Supplies for stationary center:

- colored pencils
- markers (thick and thin)
- crayons
- water pens
- small chalkboards
- colored chalk
- stencils
- alphabet stamps
- unlined writing paper of various sizes and textures
- envelopes
- stapler
- hole punch
- date stamp and stamp pad
- brass paper fasteners
- paper clips
- cellophane tape
- pencils
- rulers
- white board
- markers for the board

❖ Supplies for conferring caddy:

- "Final Draft" stamp
- date stamp
- highlighters
- folded blank books in assorted colors
- pencils
- Kindergarten Author's Planning Page (see Appendix)

❖ Supplies for publishing caddy:

- multicultural crayons and markers
- colored pencils
- scented markers
- Write-Over markers
- glitter crayons
- watercolor pencils
- bold colored markers
- crayons
- colored tissue papers
- glue
- scissors
- cut paper

❖ Supplies for each student:

Kathy gives each student a writing folder. Inside the folder, children will have reference tools such as an alphabet chart, a list of high-frequency words (which Kathy highlights in yellow when the child is able to write them using standard spelling), and a word stretcher (a thick, colored rubber band). Students will store their drafts here, too.

Make Writing Supplies Visually Appealing

Clearly label containers, with materials labeled with both words and pictures. Use writing tools that are eye-catching—children are fascinated by them. I introduce more simple supplies first, and then later in the year provide more intricate publishing materials like cut paper and tissue paper. I use them to model illustration techniques that children's book illustrators use.

—Kathy Godwin

MANAGEMENT SUGGESTIONS FOR KINDERGARTNERS

During writers' workshop, Kathy Godwin's kindergartners work at four tables. They are involved in various stages of the writing process. Kathy's grouping arrangement is based on the rotation model developed by New Zealand educator Darla Wood-Walters. Kathy names the groups as follows:

Red Bears Table—Students work on their drafts. (Some may be writing words, letters, or squiggly marks for letters which need to be interpreted.)

Green Bears Table—Students work on their drafts.

Blue Bears Table—Children write and/or confer with Kathy. Some students read their first drafts aloud, and talk about how they might revise their pieces. Some children look through their journals and choose a piece to bring to final copy. Others are preparing final copy, correcting spelling and adding information. Kathy spends a few moments with each "blue bear." During these conferences, students fill out My Conference Checklist (see Appendix). Kathy then takes the child's final draft and conferring sheet and prepares the piece for publishing by printing or typing it in the blank book of the child's choice. (Parent volunteers help with this, too.)

Yellow Bears Table—Students are in the final stages of publishing their books. They illustrate text, using materials in the portable publishing caddies.

Jane, Nate, and Zachary are busily illustrating as they publish their writing.

ORGANIZING WRITERS' WORKSHOP IN FIRST GRADE

In Lisa Holm's first-grade classroom, there are two areas devoted to writing: the writing center and the publishing center. The publishing center is a rectangular table within the writing-center area, where students illustrate their books.

❖ **Supplies for writing center:**

- a variety of children's dictionaries
- a speaking Franklin Speller
- a class word-bank dictionary

- students' writing folders
- Author's Planning Page (see Appendix)
- different types of paper: unlined, lined, and half lined/half unlined

- signs and charts, such as My First Grade Revision Checklist or Grade One Writing Criteria Chart (see Appendix)

❖ **Supplies for publishing center:**

Publishing tools, such as Write-Over markers and glitter crayons, help entice students to publish their work. Before illustrating, children type their stories into the computer and print them out. (In the beginning of the year, the teacher or a parent volunteer does this for them.)

MANAGEMENT SUGGESTIONS FOR FIRST GRADERS

Early in the year, Lisa divides her class into five writing groups. Like Kathy, she uses a modification of the Darla Wood-Walters model. Later in the year, a pocket chart (see photo) helps students keep track of which step they are on.

Like Kathy Godwin's kindergartners, each of Lisa's first graders keeps a writing folder.

At the end of writers' workshop, Lisa asks each child what he or she has accomplished and notes that in her anecdotal records. She also notes what area a child had difficulty with that day. Then, she asks each student what his/her plans are for the next day. Lisa uses this information to help her plan mini-lessons that address her students' needs.

Joel and Dorothy show how they keep track of what step of the writers' workshop they are on.

ORGANIZING WRITERS' WORKSHOP IN SECOND GRADE

In Melissa's classroom, the writing supplies reflect the greater degree of independence that second graders have, compared with kindergartners and first graders. Her students write, revise, edit, and publish with less assistance from her, relying more on peer help and checklists.

❖ **Supplies for writing center:**

- dictionaries
- Franklin Spellers
- colored pencils
- markers
- crayons
- buddy revision and

- editing checklists (see Appendix.)
- individual revision and editing checklists
- variety of paper for illustrations

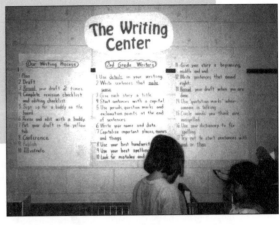

The writing center comes alive with posted writing procedures and criteria.

MANAGEMENT SUGGESTIONS FOR SECOND GRADERS

Here are ways Melissa encourages independence in her writers' workshop:

• Melissa helps students revise their work on their own by modeling the process and by conducting group revision conferences.

• She posts a sign-up sheet for buddy revision and editing conferences, as well as revision/editing conferences with her.

• Children signal they're ready for a conference with her by placing their piece in the draft basket.

• Melissa displays writing process charts and writing criteria charts in her classroom so children can use these as a reference (see Appendix).

TEACHER TIP

Colorful Paper Is Instant Motivator

"I found that when I provided a variety of colored, lined paper and gave the students choice in their selections of paper, children were motivated to write. I store my colored paper in a letter sorter (available in office-supply stores). This makes it easy for children to locate materials without teacher assistance."

—Melissa Miller

Chapter Two

The Elements *of a* Writers' Workshop

Kelly: Keisha, I've just put my name in the "editing pocket" in our writing steps chart. But when I reread my story, I realized I left out one of the most important parts of my story! It's about how the big giant got down the tree.

Keisha: Well, what are you going to do? Oh, I know! I remember. The teacher told us it's OK to go back and add stuff, even if we're in the middle of editing.

Kelly: That's right. I forgot. I'll just move my name from the "editing pocket" back to the "revising" pocket, and then I'll move it back to the "editing" pocket when I'm done.

Kelly thought that she was ready to edit her writing, but she discovered she had left out an important piece of information. Even though Kelly was at the "Editing Own Writing" step, and was checking for spelling and punctuation errors, she moved back to revise her writing by adding more details. Kelly and her classmates understand that writing is not a lockstep process.

They know that professional writers naturally move back and forth between the steps, from the time they first jot down an idea to when their work is about to go into print. Students know they can move up and down the steps, just as they can move up and down a flight of stairs.

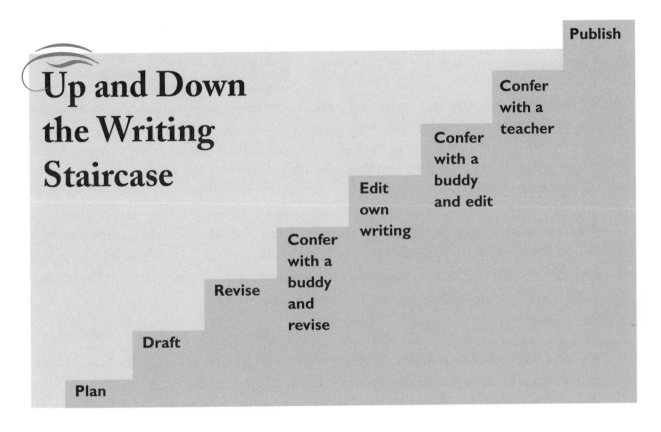

Up and Down the Writing Staircase

Plan — Draft — Revise — Confer with a buddy and revise — Edit own writing — Confer with a buddy and edit — Confer with a teacher — Publish

❖ **Plan.** Very young students plan by talking, drawing pictures, making notes, and using story planners and organizers. Dialogue may include conversations and brainstorming about experiences they have had, and discussing things they know. Drawing helps solidify their plan.

Planning is divided into two steps:

1. Choose a topic or idea.
2. Organize the information on paper by writing or drawing about it.

(Older primary students may web or list ideas and may not need to draw a picture first.)

❖ **Draft.** Very young students write text that matches and/or clarifies the picture-story they have drawn. Older primary students sometimes write their draft on every other line, so that beginning revision strategies can be implemented. In the drafting step, we encourage students to place their ideas on paper, without the constraints of perfect spelling and punctuation. (See the Developmental Stages of Writing, on page 25, for more about what to expect from students.)

❖ **Revise**. Very young students are usually revise by adding on information at the end of their writing. Older primary students can be taught how to reread their own writing and use a revision checklist (with the use of such tools as carets, asterisks, arrows, and line-outs).

After revision, Joshua Lee prepares his work for publication.

❖ **Confer with a buddy and revise.** Students may be able to read to another child what they have written. Primary children can be taught how to read their writing to a peer or to a small group, so that the peer can use a buddy revision checklist to help the writer with revision.

❖ **Edit own writing.** Very young students are not able to do this without assistance from the teacher. Older primary students can be taught how to use an editing checklist to proof-read their writing and look for spelling and punctuation errors. Individual word banks, dictionaries, and Franklin Spellers can expedite this.

❖ **Confer with a buddy and edit.** Kindergarten students are usually not able to do this. Older primary students can be taught how to use the buddy editing checklist to proofread another student's writing and look for spelling and punctuation errors (see Chapter 4 and Appendix).

❖ **Confer with teacher.** Young students are quite capable of reading their piece aloud to

Giovanna Pino confers with her teacher, Pam Simpkins.

their teacher and conferring about it. They check to make sure the piece makes sense, matches their illustration, and contains enough details. Older primary students are more adept at working with a teacher to closely examine parts of their writing, such as the beginning, middle, and end. They can also see if their title matches the story. (See Chapter 4.)

❖ **Publish.** After the children have completed a teacher/student conference, they publish their work. All published work is free of errors and is in conventional spelling (see Chapter 4).

The Developmental Stages of Writing

First-grade students in Mrs. Holm's class point to the writers' workshop steps they use.

Children learn how to experiment with writing when they observe people important to them involved in such activities. As children are exposed to books, and pretend to read, they become aware of the symbols of print on the page. As pencils, paper, crayons, markers, and paint are made available, young writers explore and make discoveries about printed symbols.

The transference of writing symbols to ideas is gradual and flows developmentally. Since stages are fluid, a child may show evidence of more than one stage in any one piece she writes. The following Developmental Stages of Writing are based on the work of Richard Gentry.

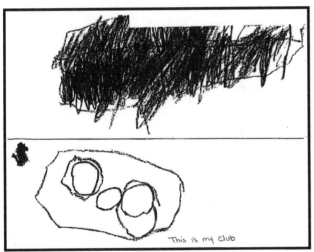

Circular scribbling. Scribbling is more notable if the student can read what the marks depict.

❖ **Scribbling.** Scribbling looks like a random assortment of marks on a child's paper. Sometimes the marks are large, circular, and random, and resemble drawing. Although the marks do not resemble print, they are significant because the young writer uses them to show ideas.

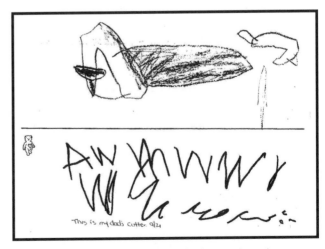

Letter-like symbols. Usually, children begin experimenting with writing the letters in their own names or family members' names.

❖ **Letter-like Symbols.** Letter-like forms emerge, sometimes randomly placed, and are interspersed with numbers. The children can tell about their own drawings or writings. In this stage, spacing is rarely present.

❖ **Strings of Letters.** In the strings-of-letters phase, students write some legible letters that tell us they know more about writing. Students are developing awareness of the sound-to-symbol relationship, although they are not matching most sounds. Students usually write in capital letters and have not yet begun spacing.

Strings of letters. In this stage, the message makes sense and matches the picture.

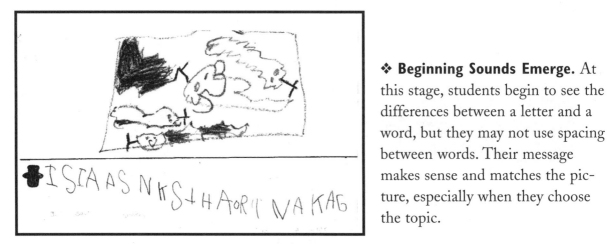

Strings of letters with some beginning sounds. Students can write down a few sounds on their own to represent words.

❖ **Beginning Sounds Emerge.** At this stage, students begin to see the differences between a letter and a word, but they may not use spacing between words. Their message makes sense and matches the picture, especially when they choose the topic.

❖ **Consonants Represent Words.** Students begin to leave spaces between their words and may often mix upper- and lowercase letters in their writing. They begin using punctuation and usually write sentences that tell ideas.

Consonants represent words. Students begin to associate sounds and consonant matches.

❖ Initial, Middle, and Final Sounds. Students in this phase may spell correctly some sight words, siblings' names, and environmental print, but other words are spelled the way they sound. Children easily hear sounds in words, and their writing is very readable.

Initial, middle, and final sounds. These students' words contain beginning, middle, and ending sounds.

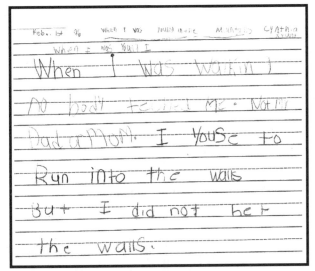

Sample of transitional phase. These students rely more consistently on visual memory and begin to notice if spelling looks right.

❖ Transitional Phases. This writing is readable and approaches conventional spelling. The students' writing is interspersed with words that are in standard form and have standard letter patterns.

❖ Standard Spelling. Students in this phase can spell most words correctly and are developing an understanding of root words, compound words, and contractions. This understanding helps students spell similar words.

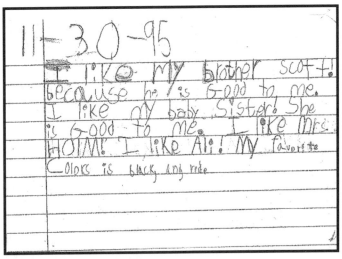

Entry from Alex's personal journal. In this piece, all of his words are in standard spelling.

Parts *of a* Writers' Workshop

At Rolling Valley school, writers' workshop can last up to one hour. The more students write, the more comfortable they are with writing, and the longer they will be able to work on their pieces. The parts of a typical workshop are:

Keisha displays her pride in publishing a flip book about George Washington.

❖ **Modeling** (approximately 10–15 minutes). Usually, the whole class or a small group addresses a skill or procedure, such as adding details to writing or conferring with class-mates. These sessions are led by the teacher or by the teacher and a student.

❖ **Writing** (approximately 30 minutes). Students work on all phases of the writing process. They may be doing any of the following: planning, drafting, revising alone or with a part-ner, editing alone or with a partner, revising or editing in a small group, conferring with the teacher, or publishing.

❖ **Sharing** (approximately 5–10 minutes). A student sits in the Author's Chair and reads aloud his writing-in-progress, as well as finished pieces. The class gives specific feedback about what was done well, asks questions about the piece, and gives suggestions for adding or deleting material.

❖ **Management** (approximately 10 minutes). The teacher asks each child what he or she accomplished during the workshop that day and what his or her plans are for the next day. The teacher records the students' responses on a class writing record sheet. If the teacher uses a pocket chart that shows the steps of the writing process, students now move their name cards to the step they will be on the next day.

Mrs. Godwin helps Nate hold his published book, as he shares it from the Author's Chair.

Getting Started *with* Writers' Workshop

There are three important questions to consider when getting your writers' workshop started. Do you have students who are afraid to take a risk in writing words they are not sure how to spell? Do you have students who over-rely on you for spelling assistance while they are writing? Do you have students who do not know how to begin their writing? The following strategies, modified from a writing conference at Lesley College, in Boston, Massachusetts, will help you address these questions and establish a positive climate with very young writers.

INTRODUCTORY LESSON FOR WRITERS' WORKSHOP

❖ **Discover what children know and care about.** Begin by brainstorming with students the names of people or things children know and care about ("my grandmother," or "my bicycle," and so forth). Write children's responses on the chalkboard. Explain to children that this list is an important one. Soon they will be writing and drawing pictures of these people or things.

❖ **Show students that temporary spelling is acceptable.** Arrange to have the school secretary, a newspaper reporter, a college student, or anyone else who uses a form of shorthand to visit the classroom and explain how she or he writes words in a special manner. This helps students see that their temporary spelling is acceptable, just as the secretary's shorthand is valuable. Experts say that if a child knows five or six beginning consonant sounds, the child is ready to participate in the writing process.

❖ **Work with a word stretcher.** Model how to write a word by stretching it with a word stretcher. A word stretcher is a thick, colored rubber band, which you place at the base of your index finger as you stretch out the sounds in words. Distribute one rubber band to each student, so they practice saying, stretching, and spelling words. The teacher leads the practice:

Alex uses a Word Stretcher to figure out how to spell his word.

"When I say d-oooooooooooo-g g g g g, what letters do you hear?

"Listen again."

Repeat the words, exaggerating the sounds. The students say *dog* in the same manner. The objective is for students to say each word slowly, and to hear the letter sounds in the word as an aid to spelling it. The students volunteer letters that they hear, and you write them on the chalkboard. Accept students' approximations. For example, if they spell it *dag,* you would say something to the effect of: "That's a very good temporary spelling for dog. Look, you heard the *d* and the *g* sounds. Good for you." Comment positively on the letters that the children correctly heard, but do not fix their errors. Then say something along the lines of, "Boys and girls, just like our secretary, who showed us an unusual way that she writes called shorthand, you also have a special way to write. It's called 'temporary spelling.'"

❖ **Students color and label.** Have students illustrate and label the people and things that they know and care about. They can work at their tables or seats figuring out the temporary spelling with their classmates. At this time, model how students can be "teachers," by assisting other classmates to hear sounds in words and to spell them.

❖ **Students share their work.** Invite students to show their "know and care about" picture to the class, and tell about what they wrote to accompany the picture.

If this lesson is too long for your students, divide it into two sessions. Plan to repeat this kind of lesson to keep students progressing and hearing the sounds of words. Each day, have children write about things they know and care about. For example, the next day, you might invite a child to draw a picture on a transparency or a chart, then label it with a word or sentence. Ask the students to name more things and people they know and care about. Brainstorm topic ideas, and then begin the writers' workshop. On subsequent days, have other children continue showing the class pictures and labels of things they care about, until children are comfortable with writing. Then, have them write stories.

Alexandra shares what she knows and cares about with Mrs. Godwin and the class.

LESSONS THAT INTRODUCE THE CONCEPT OF STORY

Once students are familiar with a daily routine of writing, they are ready to develop a story, which has a beginning, middle, and end. The following ideas meet the needs of children in grades one and two, and possibly, some in kindergarten.

❖ LESSON 1

1. Ask students what they know about the parts of a story. List these, being sure that beginning, middle, and end are mentioned.

2. Next, read a short picture book with a clear beginning, middle, and end. Show students teacher-made pictures of the beginning, middle, and end of that story, and ask why each is categorized in that manner. (*Sun up, Sun down,* by Gail Gibbons, has a clear beginning, middle, and end, and also ties into science. Other books that work well are: *Cloudy With a Chance of Meatballs* by Judi Barrett; *The Great Escape* by Eileen Christelow; and two classics, *Rosie's Walk* by Pat Hutchins and *Make Way for Ducklings* by Robert McCloskey.)

Kathy Godwin shares a story with a clear beginning, middle, and end.

Students retell *Aladdin and the Magic Lamp* graphically, pointing out the beginning, middle, and end of the book.

❖ LESSON 2

Tell a story that has a clear beginning, middle, and end. Use a graphic organizer to show the parts of a story. Read a book that has a clear beginning, middle, and end. Try *Aladdin and the Magic Lamp* by Deborah Hantzia. Use props as you read the story.

As a group, identify the beginning, middle, and end, then invite volunteers, one at a time, to fill in a graphic organizer (at the overhead projector) that has three spaces for those three parts. Now ask students to retell the story, using the graphic organizer as a guide.

On subsequent days, read aloud and discuss other books with a clear beginning, middle, and end. Gradually, introduce stories that also have problems and solutions.

❖ LESSON 3

Begin telling an original story, then stop and have a student continue the tale, using his/her own words. Be sure the child stays on-topic. That student stops at another important part, then another student continues, and so on, until the story is finished. This is fast-moving and fun. It builds imagination, improves communication skills, and strengthens the children's understanding of the elements of a story. At the end, have the class determine the beginning, middle, and end of the story. Review the problem and the solution.

❖ LESSON 4

Have students illustrate the five components of the story (beginning, middle, end, problem, and solution) on a graphic organizer. This helps children review what was learned.

❖ LESSON 5

1. Create a new class story. Have students list and vote on which topic, char-

Lizzy and Chris stamp "Draft" on the stories they are writing.

TEACHER TIP

Reinforce Problem and Solution

"To help children make the transition from recognizing a story's beginning, middle, and end to indentifying its problem and solution, too, read aloud and discuss several books that have strong problems and solutions. Some favorites are: *Chrysanthemum* by Kevin Henkes; *The Fourth Pig Escape* by Teresa Celsi; *Martha Speaks* by Susan Meddaugh; *Leo the Late Bloomer* by Robert Kraus; and *Elmer* by David McKee."

—Nancy Areglado

acters, setting, and problem they want. Students can then preplan their story with you, using a story graphic organizer that is divided into sections.

2. Ask students to tell the story.

Model how to refer back to the organizer as an aid in writing. Act as a scribe at the overhead projector, and write the story on a transparency. Encourage revision as you reread the story together. Ask:

• Does this make sense?
• Do we need to add anything?
• Is there anything that doesn't fit?

❖ LESSON 6 & BEYOND

Have students write individual stories, while you continue to read aloud stories with a clear beginning, middle, end, problem, and solution. Provide students with "My Question Planner Sheet" (see sample, right). Show students how to use this as a guide for their writing. Post additional questions, such as those listed above. Ask each child to reread his or her draft, and ask him- or herself the revision questions.

Name _____

Date _____

My Question Planner Sheet

Who? _____
_____

When? _____
_____

Where? _____
_____

What Happens? _____
_____

Why? _____
_____

Mrs. Miller's class works on the drafts of their stories.

❖ LESSON 7

Introduce the importance of details in writing. Show students two teacher-made books, one with many vivid details, the other with few. Ask students to comment on the differences between the stories, and then invite them to brainstorm several writing topics, listing possible details for each idea. Did one topic lend itself to more details? Might that be the one you care about most? Ask students to tell you which topics they would like to make into stories. Distribute blankbooks and "My Story Planner Sheet" (right) to each child. Discuss how to use the story organizer, and have children complete it before writing.

LITERATURE AS A CATALYST FOR WRITING

Children's literature can be used to spark students' writing. In fact, some literature can stimulate in children ideas for good stories of their own.

At the beginning of the year, we use Cynthia Rylant's Caldecott-winning *When I Was Young in the Mountains*. As students listen to the author recall her growing-up years in the mountains, they begin to think of good times they had when they were "young." Nancy Areglado, for example, invites kindergarten students to write a class big book. Each child illustrates a page and fills in "When I was young, I _____."

First-grade teacher Lisa Holm uses *Begin at the Beginning*, by Amy Schwartz, to introduce topic choice in writing. The story centers on Sara, a girl who can't figure out what to paint for the art show. As the story goes on, Sara realizes that she can paint what she knows: the tree outside her window. Lisa Holm uses the book to emphasize that when students write what they know well, they'll have a wealth of topics from which to choose.

For Kathy Godwin, books about writing help her kindergartners appreciate the importance of choosing rich topics. Says Kathy, "I read aloud *Joy Cowley Writes* to the class. Cowley says that when she writes stories, she works hard at rewriting to 'make the story as good as I can get it.' Cowley also says 'an idea for a story is like a little seed. I plant it in my imagina-

---

Name _____

Date _____

My Story Planner Sheet

Who? (the characters) _____

_____

When? Where? (the setting) _____

_____

What happens? (problem and solution) _____

_____

Beginning	Middle	End

Kathy Godwin helps Joshua make his story "as good as he can get it."

tion. Sometimes it grows. Sometimes it doesn't grow.' My students understand this, especially since they plant seeds in class and watch them grow. They excitedly chime in with anecdotes about how ideas for their stories originate. I explain to students that Cowley writes her story first, just to get the idea, then rewrites extensively, until the story is just right. I point out that the way Cowley works as a writer is the same as they can work. This motivates my students to begin their stories, and to revise."

TEACHER TIP

The Power of Personal Journals

"When my first graders come into the classroom, they check the board for warm-up activities. Three times a week, the warm-up activity is 'Write in Your Personal Journal.' During the first week of school, I model for the children by writing in my own personal journal, which is a simple composition notebook. I might write about something that happened to me that morning, a family anecdote, an activity I enjoy, or an event I'm planning. I invite students to make comments or ask questions.

The next week, the children begin writing in their own journals. Sometimes a child wants to write a private entry, so I tell the class to mark private entries with a star. That way, others—including me—know not to read that part.

After the class has written for 10–20 minutes, I invite volunteers to share their writing with classmates. Those sharing are invited to go to the front of the room and sit in the Writer's Rocker (a child-size rocker), while they read their entry aloud. The Writer's Rocker has tremendous appeal, and we never have a shortage of volunteers!"

—Lisa Holm

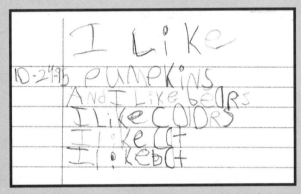

An October sample of Alex's personal journal.

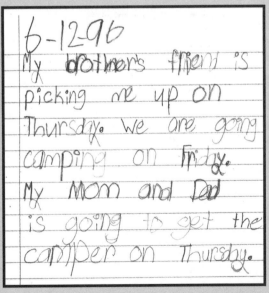

A look at Alex's June entry shows his amazing growth in composing skills and mechanics.

Constructing a Criteria Chart

Your children need an awareness of the standards of good writing. You can encourage this by discussing the criteria for effective writing, then developing a criteria chart together.

Begin by gathering samples that illustrate effective writing. (Use student samples from a previous year, or generate some yourself.) On the overhead projector, display a well-written sample and a weak sample. Here is a typical dialogue:

Mrs. Holm: Today we'll look at two first-grade writing samples, and we'll brainstorm what each writer did well. I'll write down all the things that you say are examples of good writing. Let's look at the first sample. What did this student do well?

Today is my brthday! I can't wate to get hom! I'm having my frendz over for my parti. We're going to make a gigantk snowman and then ete cak and ice krem.

Libby: He put a stop sign at the end of the sentence.
Mrs. Holm: Yes, that's right! What is another name for a stop sign at the end of a sentence?
Libby: A period.
Mrs. Holm: Excellent! Is this a sentence that asks us or tells us something?
Michael: It tells us that the boy will make a snowman with his friends.
Mrs. Holm: That's right. Let's write about telling sentences and periods on our writing chart. What should we write? When do we use a period?
Ali: We can use a stop sign at the end of a sentence that tells us something.
Mrs. Holm: Great suggestion. [Teacher writes the criterion in the student's words.] Now, let's look back at the sample. What else about the sample shows good writing?

The teacher continues the lesson, adding new criteria as suggested by the class. The chart is posted for the children to refer to as they compose their writing. Additional criteria are added each time a new writing strategy is taught, such as how to make sense in a piece.

As the year goes on, and children learn about revising and editing, the class rewrites the chart into two separate sections, one for revising and one for editing. Revising is considered "anything that would make your paper sound better or make more sense."

Editing is defined as "anything that would make your paper look better, even remembering to write your name and the date."

At first, writers may notice only the mechanics of writing. But you can guide students to notice elements of content, too, such as using details or staying on-topic. The charts are used by students as a tool when they evaluate writing samples for portfolio assessment.

Chapter Three

Writing with Precision, Writing with a Plan

The more children see that writing plays an important part in their school lives and in connecting them to others, the more they love writing and the more they will write. It's up to us as teachers to give children lots of opportunities to write for real purposes and specific audiences, to help them know they are members of what Frank Smith calls "The Literacy Club."

And often, the impetus to write for a purpose comes from children. When Mary Dill purchased dry-erase boards for each primary class in the school, students were so thankful, they wanted to write notes to Mrs. Dill. And they did—with the help of their teacher, who showed them how to write a letter.

When Nancy Areglado lived in Massachusetts, her first graders decided to write Eric Carle, in the form of a big book, *Eric Carle—This Is Your Life*. Nancy purchased ten sheets of white poster board and enlisted the art teacher to help children illustrate in Carle's tissue-paper-collage style. The children wrote the biography, closing up the book with thoughts on what makes his work so special. When Eric Carle received the book, he sent Nancy's class a personal note on his *Hungry*

Hungry Caterpillar stationery, telling them he was so excited about the book, he had it on display in his studio. He also sent the children pieces of tissue paper he used to illustrate his books.

The children's excitement was hard to contain. They wrote for a specific purpose for a specific audience, who confirmed the value of their undertaking.

Inspired events like that are not an everyday occurrence. It's more often the case that we have to jump start our students' imaginations to find compelling writing ideas. Here are some strategies for doing just that.

Strategies *for* Sparking Ideas

❖ **Play Turn-Pair-Share.** Lisa Holm asks her students to pair up with a buddy—by sitting cross-legged and knee-to-knee—and share. She gives them specific directions for sharing, such as "Tell your buddy about a pet you have or a pet you would like to have." Says Lisa, "During the minute to a minute-and-a-half of share time, the children talk with animation. When the timer beeps, they turn and face the front of the classroom. I ask, 'Who would like to share what your buddy told you?'"

After students share, they return to their seats and either work on a story in progress or begin a new story, "bursting with new ideas."

Students in Mrs. Holm's class share ideas during Turn-Pair-Share.

❖ **Turn artifacts into art.** Make your classroom rich with collectibles (personal treasures and photos you and students have brought in). Draw out the stories behind these artifacts, and encourage children to write about

Students are ready to share their ideas with the class.

them with comments such as "Oh, that would make a great story!" As Malcolm Cowley says, "Although each writer's process is idiosyncratic, each writer begins with a precious particle and then grows meaning from it." It's our responsibility to help children to see that there are story seeds ready to blossom all around us.

❖ **Write about what you know.** Steven Shepard, an author at age thirteen, spoke to an audience of students at Rolling Valley and had this to say in response to a student's question about how he got his story ideas.

"I'll tell you what my father told me a long time ago when I began writing, and it has worked for me ever since. He said, 'Just write what you know!' So, I started thinking. I know about kids my age, I know about fishing, and I know about the coast of Maine, because I spend my summers there. I'll just write a book about a boy my age who gets stranded in the middle of a mist of fog. That's how I got the ideas for my book *Fogbound.*"

❖ **Magic glasses, magic ears.** Kalli Dakos, author of several hilarious books of poetry about school, advised students at Rolling Valley to "put on your magic glasses and your magic ears, because you never know when there is a story or poem lurking around the corner." To prove her point, she mentioned she was talking to Mrs. Dill, the school principal, about one of her poems about bugs. Mrs. Dill laughed and said, "Kalli, I don't like bugs — not even crickets." Kalli enthusiastically replied, "That would make a wonderful poem." "The Principal Who Doesn't Do Bugs" will be published in one of Kalli's new poetry books.

❖ **Inspiring swap talk.** Nancy Areglado gathered a class of first-grade students around her on the "circle time" rug. She had just finished a mini-lesson on the elements of a story. Then it was time for the students to decide on a topic for their stories. Some seemed stumped, so Ms. Areglado modeled the following:

"Let's brainstorm some ideas for stories. I have an idea for a story of my own. I'm going to write about how my dog, Morgan, puts a teddy bear in her mouth every time the doorbell rings. That's how she happily greets visitors to our house.

"I'll pick this beautiful blue book to write my story in. Now, who has an idea for a story? As soon as you share your idea, you can select your special book."

After students tell their topic and choose their blank books, they jump into their writing. Students who are searching for good topics hear others suggest suitable ones, and this stimulates their own writing.

I-Can-Write-About Sheets

"When I hear children say, 'I don't know what to write about,' it's time for a 'perk-up-my-writing-with-new-ideas'

Joshua, a kindergarten student, has a number of topics to write about.

Joey begins making the illustrations for "I Can Write About."

lesson. I ask my students to share possible topics, and they enthusiastically volunteer their choices. I list their responses on a chart, and we draw pictures to accompany each suggestion. I model how to fill out the 'I Can Write About _____' sheet, by drawing pictures of topics I've listed. Then, I distribute the 'I Can Write About _____' sheets to individual students, and they color and label their choices. New ideas abound!" —Kathy Godwin

Strategies *for* Planning Stories

HAVE I GOT A PROBLEM FOR YOU!

Melissa Miller helps children build problem-and-solution structures into their stories by describing how she found a solution to a problem she once had—a car that wouldn't start.

Says Melissa: "Call a garage? Look under the hood? I thought out loud in front of the class, and explained the eventual solution. Then I related my experience to picture books that have problems and solutions, such as *The Spider and the King* by Carol Kruger; *The Schoolyard Mystery* by Elizabeth Levy; and *The Birthday Present* by Virginia King. I also read aloud the chapter 'Spring,' from *Frog and Toad Are Friends* by Arnold Lobel, and asked the group to complete a story map. They filled in the characters and setting, and, of course, the problem

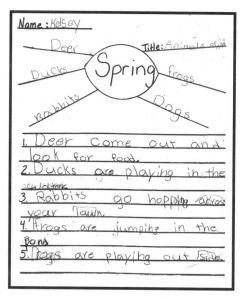

Kelsey chose to write a story map about animals in the spring.

Kelsey has published "Animals of Spring" in a flip book.

and solution. Then the children completed story maps for the books they're reading independently. When it's time to write an original story, the children find it easy, since they've had experience with several story maps."

WEB IT!

Have students write their topic in the center of the web and supporting information on the branches. Sometimes, teachers of very young children modify the traditional web by shortening it, such as the example below. This is an example of a rewrite of the book *When I Was Young in the Mountains* by Cynthia Rylant.

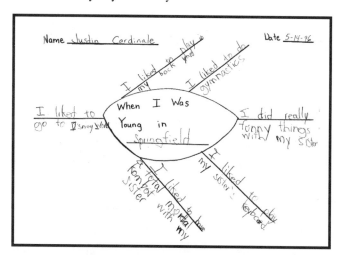

Justin planned his story, "When I Was Young in Springfield," by using a web.

Justin wrote and illustrated six pages in his published book, entitled "When I Was Young in Springfield."

STORY ORGANIZER

Prior to beginning their drafts, young children can color or write their ideas in each section of a story organizer. Story organizers can have sections for Beginning, Middle, and End. Later, Problem and Solution can be added. A more detailed example of a story organizer includes: Title, Setting, Characters, Beginning, Middle, and End.

This second grader used organizers in planning for his dinosaur project.

| Name_____ Date_____ |
| My Story Organizer |
| Beginning |
| Middle |
| End |
| Problem |
| Solution |

An example of a story organizer.

TEACHER MODELING

We do plenty of modeling, so students see examples of how to draft a piece. Here are two possible approaches.

❖ **Conduct a think-aloud.** Nancy Areglado writes a story while she thinks aloud the steps. At the overhead projector, Ms. Areglado talks about possible story choices. She'll say:

"Let's see, I'll make a list of topics. I could write about my three children, Kimberly, Julie, or Kristin. But I could also write about my golden retriever, Morgan, or my cat, Natasha. I think I'll write about how I went skiing with my dog, Morgan. Now, I'll use my story organizer to help me plan my writing."

Ms. Areglado begins drafting the piece while referring to the organizer that she filled in earlier.

"I'm not sure how to begin, so I'll look back to my organizer for ideas. Oh! I know. I'll start by saying that last week the Washington, D.C. area was blanketed with ten inches of snow. Schools were closed.

"I'll skip every other line, so I can reread what I've written and fix things that need to be changed. I'll keep looking back to my organizer to make sure I remembered to add all of my ideas."

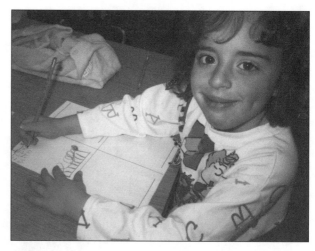

Arielle embarks on writing another story!

Ms. Areglado continues to model how rereading is an important key to the drafting process. She also demonstrates how to use a caret and an asterisk to clarify and add information.

Later, she uses the same piece and teaches revision, editing, and keyboarding to bring it to final copy. She places the story in the children's library, so it can be read during D.E.A.R. (Drop Everything And Read) time.

❖ **Write as a group.** In this approach, the teacher leads the group to create a story together.

Ms. Areglado: What shall we write about?
Josephine: Sledding!
Elcides: A black bear!
Kate: A dinosaur!
Susie: Our class going sledding!
Puneet: Our class going sledding with our teacher!
Ms. Areglado: We have quite a list of topics. How can we choose?
Josephine: Can we vote?

This they do. The class decides to write about going sledding. Ms. Areglado introduces a story organizer, and the students go to the overhead projector and draw the main parts of the story: Beginning, Middle, End, Problem, and Solution.

Ms. Areglado: You did an excellent job filling in our story organizer. Now we know the main parts of our story. If we keep looking back at the organizer and asking ourselves questions, we will know how to start our lead sentence. What comes at the beginning of the story?
Puneet: It was about our class deciding to go sledding on that big hill at Irving Intermediate School.
Ms. Areglado: That sounds terrific, Puneet. Who can think of a lead sentence?
Susie: We had so much snow, our class decided to go sledding on the big hill.
Ms. Areglado: Great, Susie! I'll write that now. How should I begin writing?
Alex: With a capital letter.
Ms. Areglado: That's right, Alex.

As the students continue dictating, Ms. Areglado guides them in looking back at the Story Organizer for additional ideas.

She shows how to reread the draft to see if it makes sense and sounds right. Next, she demonstrates how to proofread for spelling and punctuation errors. Finally, she and the students bring the story to final copy and place it in the classroom library.

Story organizer drawn by students and used as an aid in writing the story.

Drafting: Problems *and* Solutions

Once students at Rolling Valley have selected their topics, many start their stories right away. However, other children hesitate because they don't know how to begin their piece or they don't know how to spell some, or all, of the words. For this reason, some children spend an inordinate amount of time on the drawing phase. Of course, the drawing phase is an important prewriting activity, because it stimulates ideas for drafts. However, drafting should lead to the production of a written piece, too. How do teachers at Rolling Valley encourage their children to write? Here are some common problems and our solutions.

SPENDING TOO MUCH TIME ON DRAWING AND TOO LITTLE TIME ON WRITING

In Lisa Holm's first-grade class, several students dwelled on the drawing phase and ran out of time to write. Lisa solved the problem by removing some of the enticing tools in the writing center, such as Write-Over markers, scented markers, and multicultural crayons. (She moved these special supplies to the publishing center.) With everyday tools before them, such as crayons and pencils, the children were more inclined to write stories.

BEGINNING THE DRAFT IN THE WRONG PLACE ON THE PAPER

Kindergarten teacher Kathy Godwin made sure that the children's writing paper invited both writing and drawing. She divided the paper in half horizontally, and placed a picture of

This kindergarten student found the teddy-bear marker helpful.

a teddy bear in the left corner under the dividing line. The teddy bear signified the place where the students were to begin writing. This technique helped students focus on both drawing and writing.

NOT KNOWING HOW TO BEGIN THE FIRST SENTENCE

To help some second graders get started, Melissa Miller asked some children a series of leading questions about their topic. ("Your story is about your puppy? What do you and your puppy like to do?") After listening to their responses, she discussed with them possible ways to begin.

STUCK ON SPELLING WORDS CORRECTLY

When students are stuck on spelling, they often have trouble getting ideas down on paper. To help a child who's stuck, ask the child to say the word as he claps the syllables. This helps the child think of the sounds in each syllable, one at a time. Spelling the whole word becomes less overwhelming. Also model the word stretcher—a thick rubber band which the child can stretch while slowly saying the word aloud.

Arielle shows how the word stretcher helps her spell words while she is writing.

TOO DEPENDENT ON YOU FOR SPELLING

To help children become more independent with spelling, encourage them to consult spelling resources such as Word Walls, Word Bank cards, alphabet cards (with pictures of each beginning letter), a speaking Franklin Speller, student-made dictionaries, a commercial dictionary, and a criteria chart for strategies that help students spell words.

TRYING TO WRITE WITH THE WRONG DRAFT PAPER

Consultant Darla Wood-Walters stresses that providing the right size draft paper is an important element for helping children write. For example, students who have weak small-motor skills enjoy writing on blank paper without lines. Students who are able to write some letters are better suited for paper that contains primary lines on the bottom half and a picture section at the top, so students can draw a picture as part of

Dana chooses just the right kind of paper from the writing center.

rehearsal. The bottom part of this paper contains dotted lines in the middle of every two solid lines, and those lines are larger than normal. The large lines help young writers maintain better control over their small muscles. Finally, for children who have good small-motor skills, primary-lined paper with narrower lines (with no space for a picture) is a good choice. (The entire sheet consists of alternating solid and dotted lines.) It's just right for fluent writers.

DIFFICULTY WITH HANDWRITING

The computer can be a boost for kids who have trouble with handwriting. These students can be taught keyboarding basics. It's often beneficial to have parent volunteers available for added support and encouragement. Gradually, students can plan, draft, revise, edit, and write final copies on the computer. Some beginners may use the computer for the final copy only.

NO ROOM ON THE DRAFT FOR MAKING EDITS

We encourage students to reread their drafts to make sure the pieces make sense and sound right. Sometimes, however, children recognize that a section needs work, but there is no place on the page to revise. For this reason, we encourage students to write their drafts on every other line, building in space for revision.

Chapter Four

Encourage Children to Revise, Edit, Confer and Publish

How can we awaken in students a desire to make their writing, in the words of Joy Cowley, "as good as I can get it"? Our secret to teaching young students to revise and edit is to model techniques in a variety of ways. With teacher modeling, all students are exposed to the process, and many grasp the elements of good writing.

In this chapter, we will share classroom-tested techniques for teaching editing, revision, conferring, and publishing.

REVISING AND EDITING IN KINDERGARTEN

Kathy Godwin says: "Revision conferences are at the heart of teaching children about editing and revising their work. I start a revision conference by asking the child to share her picture, then share her writing. We talk about how to add one or two words to make a sentence sound better and make more sense. Also, I point out that by adding another thought, a piece can be of greater interest to the reader. Here's a sample exchange with a child who has mastered many skills:

Joey and Giovanna read Kinder Express stories.

Teacher: I can see from your picture that you have a plate of food on the table. Would you like to read your writing to me?

Student: Sure! It says, "I like healthy foods!"

Teacher: That's wonderful, Arielle. Can you tell me what you put at the end of your sentence?

Student: It's an exclamation point.

Teacher: What does an exclamation point tell us?

Student: Something exciting!

Teacher: You heard lots of sounds in your words.

Student: I did! I also remembered to put spaces between my words.

Teacher: Nice work. Are there any changes you would like to make?

Student: I want to add, "because they're good for you."

Teacher: Where would you add that?

Student: Here. *[Arielle points to the middle of her sentence.]*

Teacher: What do we do when we add more details between our words?

Student: We put a caret. It looks just like this! *[Arielle draws a caret and writes her new addition.]*

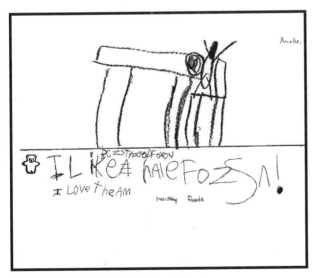

Arielle's revision, done with Mrs. Godwin.

Arielle's final copy.

KINDERGARTEN REVISION EXPECTATIONS

During kindergarten, students are beginning to read their writing to classmates and teachers, as well as listen to hear if their writing makes sense. At this time, some students—with teacher modeling and coaching—are able to add one to two descriptive words or extend an idea to make their writing more interesting. As the year progresses and students become accustomed to the revision process, they begin to develop their ideas more independently.

During midyear, the revision symbols "line-out" and "caret" are introduced through teacher modeling. Some students will use these symbols with coaching in the revision process. Between midyear and the end of the year, students will dictate/write a title to go along with their writing. By the end of the year, students are becoming proficient at reading their own writing and deciding if it makes sense.

REVISING AND EDITING IN FIRST GRADE

For first and second grades, you can teach your children to hold small-group revision conferences, as described on pages 53 and 54 of this book.

Lisa Holm's first graders show a range of revision abilities. By the middle of the year, some children are adept at revising their own work. Some are even able to help others revise, or can do so by the middle or end of the year. Still other first graders are not able to revise at all, and struggle with this until the end of the year.

Some children can edit a group story with the teacher, but are not yet ready to edit their own work. Other children can do so easily, especially with an editing checklist, but are not able to do so with partners.

FIRST-GRADE REVISION EXPECTATIONS

At the beginning of the year, students will:

❖ read what he/she has written.
❖ determine if writing makes sense.
❖ begin to use line-out to remove unwanted words.
❖ dictate/write additions to writing.
❖ dictate/write a title for writing.

Midyear, the student will:

❖ read what he/she has written.
❖ determine if writing makes sense.
❖ use line-out to remove unwanted words.

By end of year, students will:

❖ use caret mark to add words to writing
❖ begin using asteriks and arrows to add information in writing
❖ begin using paragraph marks to signal the beginning of a new paragraph
❖ write a title that matches the writing
❖ reread what has been written to determine whether additions/changes make sense.

REVISING AND EDITING IN SECOND GRADE

A month into the school year, Melissa Miller's students are able to revise with a buddy. They may not be experts in adding details or revising for clarity, but they are developing these skills rapidly.

At the beginning of the year, students revise by adding one- or two-word details. By the end of the year, students can make their stories interesting by adding even more details.

Melissa sharpens her students' revision skills by modeling the process throughout the day. "I model revision as often as possible," says Melissa. "For example, as we write on the chalkboard, at the overhead projector, or on a chart, we model how to reread what has been written, asking:

❖ Does this make sense?
❖ Do we need to add anything?
❖ Is there anything that doesn't fit that we need to take out?

"Students gradually understand that it is important to read over what they write. This is a major breakthrough for our children, because many think that once something is written, it cannot be changed."

Melissa hangs a revision chart in a strategic location so that it is continually visible. She and her students add to the chart as they learn to work with new revision marks.

MARK		USED FOR:
Caret	∧	Put in extra information.
Asterisk	*	Add information when it doesn't fit (add info in another place).
Arrow	→	Point to where the reader should go to, after information has been changed.
Line Out	——	Cross out something.
Paragraph	¶	Signal a new paragraph.

Use Colored Pencils

"I invite my students to revise and edit using colored pencils. To do so, the children circle the incorrectly spelled words with the colored pencil of their choice. That makes the word easy to spot when they're rewriting the piece for final copy."

—Melissa Miller

Phillip and Justin show how peer revision and editing are done in Mrs. Miller's class.

SECOND-GRADE REVISION EXPECTATIONS

At the beginning of the year, students will:

❖ develop revision criteria with my help.

❖ practice rereading each piece two times to look for and fix mistakes.

❖ begin buddy revision by reading pieces to a partner and by working together to add details.

By the middle of the year, students will:

❖ use revision and editing checklists with my guidance.

❖ begin to use revision and editing checklists independently to fix mistakes.

❖ work with partners during buddy revision conferences.

By the end of the year, students will:

❖ use checklists independently.

❖ work fluently with peers to edit and revise.

By the end of the year, Kelly and Alex are proficient writers, editors, and publishers.

Five Steps to Teaching Revision

STEP 1. MODEL PEER REVISION CONFERENCE

One lesson that's quite effective is for two teachers to role-play a conference on revision. For example, one teacher (Ms. Areglado) plays the part of the student while Mrs. Dill plays the teacher. The lesson starts as Ms. Areglado asks Mrs. Dill to read aloud two sentences in a story. The story clearly needs revision:

Second-grade teacher Melissa Miller works in a small group with peer revisers. As children revise with a partner, Melissa may join them and assess their performance.

My plant is a turtle plant. It grows slowly, but it helps a lot.

Through questioning, the "teacher" shows the "student" how and where to add information and how to determine the best places to insert a caret and an asterisk.

Children find it humorous to see a teacher as student, but also absorb the main point of how to revise for clarity and sense.

STEP 2. DISCUSS CRITERIA FOR PEER REVISION

Then the teachers resume their roles again as teachers. They turn to the class and ask what children noticed. As a group, they set up criteria for peer revision, such as:
   ❖ Watch and listen as your partner reads the story.
   ❖ Tell your partner what he/she did well.
   ❖ See if the piece makes sense.
   ❖ See if the piece needs more details.
   ❖ See if anything needs to be taken out.

STEP 3. TEACH OLDER STUDENTS TO HOLD CONFERENCES

The teacher instructs older students how to hold a conference with a younger child, and with a group. She models the procedure until she's confident that the older students are comfortable and competent in this area.

Guidelines for Cross-Grade Revision

WITH ONE PEER

Watch and listen as your young friend reads his or her writing.

❖ Tell what is terrific! Write your comments. Make suggestions. Ask questions about things you don't understand.

❖ Ask your friend where to add details or line-out extra information. Show the writer, if necessary.

❖ Give your written comments to your friend.

❖ Summarize the things your friend did well.

IN SMALL GROUPS

Follow this procedure with each child in the group, one at a time.

❖ Watch and listen as your young friend reads his writing. Make sure your friend holds the paper so the whole group can see it.

❖ Invite each group member to tell what he or she thinks is terrific about the piece. Write down the comments.

❖ Ask the group if they have any questions for the writer, or if anything needs to be added or lined-out. Record their comments.

❖ Ask the writer where the suggested changes can be made. Show the writer, if necessary.

❖ Summarize suggestions and compliments. Give the writer the comment sheets that you created during the conference.

❖ Ask for the next volunteer and continue until all members have had a turn.

STEP 4. USE QUESTION WORDS

Lisa Holm writes these question words on cards, then displays them on the chalkboard: Who, What, When, Where, Why, and How.

Then she sets the purpose for the lesson by telling the students that they should use the question words to help them determine:

❖ what information is already in a story.

❖ what needs to be added.

Lisa has the children read the question words aloud, then invites one student to stand beside the question words and read his writing with the class. The child decides if each question, read one at a time, has been answered in the piece.

TEACHER TIP

Reaching All Learners

"To reach children who learn well graphically and kinesthetically, make a chart and divide it into two columns. Label the left column "In My Story." Label the right column "Needs to Be in My Story."

Then lead a conversation like this:

Mrs. Holm: Alex, does your writing tell who the story is about?

Alex: Yes! My story is about me and my brother, Scott.

Mrs. Holm: Under which column on the chart would you place "Who": "In My Story" or "Needs to Be in My Story"?

Alex: It goes under "In My Story," because I told who was in my story.

—Lisa Holm

DRAFT

Name Kelly Date 5-21-96

Who? Susi

What? Play

When? Resess
Where? Play ground

How? We like each other
Why? Were best friends

Kelly used the question word planner prior to writing her story.

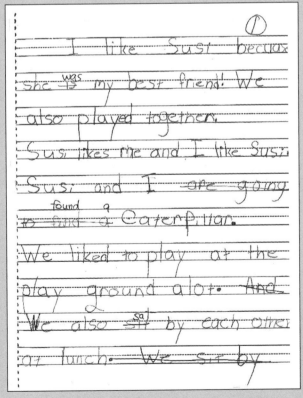

Kelly's draft, showing added revisions.

STEP 5. INTRODUCE THE FISHBOWL TECHNIQUE

Ms. Areglado taught this lesson to Lisa Holm's first-grade class.

Part of the class is in a small group at the front of the room with the teacher. They are in the fishbowl. The rest, in their seats, have been given a purpose for listening, such as, "As you watch the students in the small group revise this story, write how you would revise it. Jot down the changes that you think should be made. At the close of the lesson, we'll review what you wrote." Then the audience watches the "fishbowl lesson."

Ms. Areglado writes a story on the overhead projector. The story does not make sense.

> My plant is bad because it helps people. I don't like it.

Ms. Areglado: I've noticed that we need more practice on revising to make sense. Today we'll see how many revision strategies we can use to do that. Let's begin by rereading our chart "Our Revision Marks." How many of you have already used some of these marks when revising your work?

Monica: I've used a caret to add things.

Ms. Areglado: Terrific, Monica!

Dorothy: I've used an arrow.

Ms. Areglado: It's fun to add arrows. You can add more information than if you just used a caret. Good for you, Dorothy.

Kevin: I've used a star.

Ms. Areglado: Wonderful, Kevin. Sometimes, we call the star an asterisk.

It sounds like you already know quite a lot about revision. Now, let's read over our "My First Grade Revision Checklist," to see if there is anything else we know how to do.

Ms. Areglado tells the students that, for this lesson, they should think about carets, line-outs, arrows, and asterisks.

Referring to the story on the chart, the following exchange takes place:

Samantha: We need to get rid of *bad*. How can a plant be *bad* if it helps people?

Ms. Areglado: That certainly makes sense, Samantha. What do we call the writing term when we get rid of something?

Samantha: Line-out. I'll line-out *bad*, then I'll write *good* above it.

Ms. Areglado: Wonderful job, Samantha! Let's read it over now, with Samantha's revision. Let's see if anything else should be revised.

This they do. Another child raises his hand.

Alex: I think we need to line-out *don't*. It just doesn't make sense.

Ms. Areglado: Let's reread it including Alex's suggestion, then raise our hands if we agree with the changes.

The students agree with Alex. Kasey adds an asterisk. She also adds, "A lot of the time" after "My plant is good." The final copy reads, "My plant is good a lot of the time because it helps people. I like it."

At the close of the lesson, the audience—who was watching the fishbowl lesson—share the changes that they feel should have been made. For example, Libby adds a section at the end telling how her plant helps people. Ms. Areglado uses this as a teaching point: "Sometimes, there is more than one way to revise," she says. "Many of us have different ideas, and all of our ideas are important."

The procedures in this lesson are repeated with different students, using different samples over a number of days, until all of Mrs. Holm's first-grade students have a chance to be part of the fishbowl.

Tip: Videotape the lessons to share with the children, their parents, and other teachers.

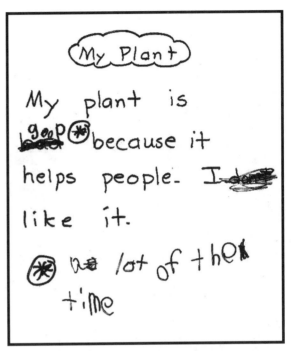

Overhead copy showing students' revisions from videotaped lesson.

STEP 6. INTRODUCE REVISION CHECKLIST FOR INDEPENDENT USE

Based on actual lessons with the children, Nancy Areglado, Lisa Holm, and Melissa Miller designed a revision checklist and an editing checklist that students could use on their own (see Appendix). The children were familiar with the information in the checklist, because they had been exposed to the items during previous lessons. Mrs. Holm found that one effective way to introduce the revision checklist was through teacher modeling. She taught the children in cooperative groups, then she let them work independently. Here are the steps she took:

Part One: She models at the front of the room how to revise a piece (which needs work) by using the revision checklist.

Part Two: She introduces another piece of writing, which also needs work. She divides the class into cooperative groups. Each group has a revision checklist and a copy of the new piece.

Part Three: She focuses on a social skill for the cooperative group, such as, "Listen to what others are saying." She asks the group: "How would a group sound and look if the children were listening to what others were saying?"

Part Four: She appoints roles: the reader (person who reads the piece), editor (person who takes the group's ideas about revision and revises directly on the piece), recorder (the person who records the group's ideas onto the revision checklist), and encouragers (people in the group who say encouraging comments about responses). She asks groups to revise.

Part Five: She takes notes about children's social skills and academic performance. She asks a representative from each group to demonstrate, at the overhead projector, how their group revised the piece.

Part Six: This lesson is repeated as many times as is necessary, using different pieces to revise. If the children are ready, she asks them to revise their own pieces independently.

A Look At One Student's Revision Process

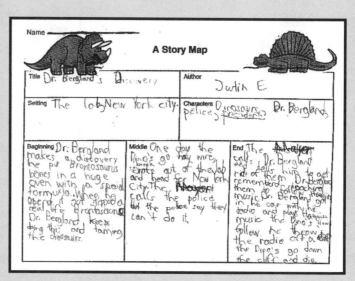

Justin's Story Map (a story-elements planner)

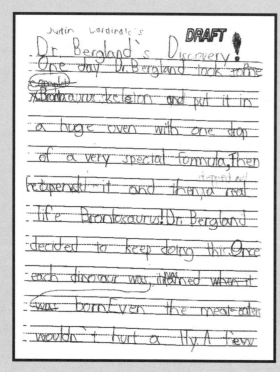

Justin's story, showing revisions.

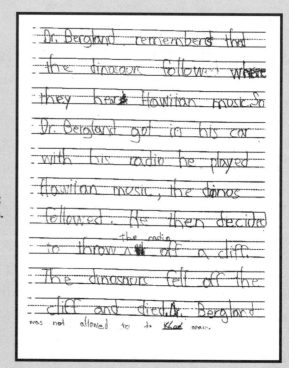

Name __Justin E__   Date _____

My Revision Checklist

	Yes	No	I fixed it.
1. Does my writing **make sense**?	√		
2. Does it **sound right**?	√		
3. Do I have enough **details**?	√√		
4. Do I have a **beginning, middle, and end**?	√		
5. Does my **title** match the story?	√		

Remember: If you answered **no** to any of the questions, add or take out information until your story **makes sense**.

Buddy's Name __Waris__   Date __4-11-96__

Buddy Revision Checklist

	Yes	No	We fixed it.
1. Does my writing **make sense**?	√		
2. Does it **sound right**?	√		
3. Do I have enough **details**?	√		
4. Do I have a **beginning, middle, and end**?	√		
5. Does my **title** match the story?	√		

Remember: If your buddy answered **no** to any of the questions, work together to fix your writing.

Name __Justin E__   Date __4-3-96__

My Editing Checklist

	Yes	No	I fixed it.
1. Did I end each sentence with a **period, exclamation point,** or **question mark**?	√		
2. Did I start each sentence with a **capital letter**?	√		
3. Did I use **quotation marks** to show when someone is talking?	√		
4. Did I use my **dictionary** to check my spelling?	√		
5. Did I **circle** any words I think are misspelled?	√		

Remember: If you answered **no** to any of the questions, try your best to fix your mistakes.

Buddy's Name __Waris__   Date __4-11-96__

Buddy Editing Checklist

	Yes	No	We fixed it.
1. Did I end each sentence with a **period, exclamation point,** or **question mark**?	√		
2. Did I start each sentence with a **capital letter**?	√		
3. Did I use **quotation marks** to show when someone is talking?	√		
4. Did I use my **dictionary** to check my spelling?		√	√
5. Did I **circle** any words I think are misspelled?	√		

Remember: If your buddy answered **no** to any of the questions, work together to fix your mistakes.

Justin's final copy of his dinosaur story.

STEP 7. INTRODUCE A COMMITTEE OF REVISERS

We find that, within a classroom, no matter how many focus lessons we do, some students do not understand how to revise. To help them, we appoint a team of student revisers, who give one-on-one assistance. The job is rotated, and those working in that position during writers' workshop wear washable plastic visors labeled "Revisers." Revisers begin with a compliment about the child's piece; use four revision marks: arrows, carets, asterisks, and line-outs; write suggestions on Post-its only, not on the piece, since the final decision to revise belongs to the writer.

STEP 8. SHOW HOW TO REVISE ENDINGS

Here's an overview of how we teach children to revise the endings to their work.

❖ Part One: Make an Analogy.

Ms. Areglado tells students in Mrs. Miller's class why writing and revising endings reminds her of taking a plane ride. She asks students how many have flown in a jet. They comment on how it feels to take off, to stay on-course, and to land.

Ms. Areglado: Writing a story or a piece of information is like taking a plane ride. You begin with an energizing lead, stay on-course by staying on-topic, and add details about the trip or the topic. When we come in for a landing, is it a crash landing or is it a smooth landing that eases down the runway?

Susan: It's a smooth landing.

Ms. Areglado: That's right! So we want to see how we can prepare the reader that our paper is coming to a close, just as we are prepared for a landing when we hear the landing gear being lowered.

• If you'd like to let readers know that the ending is coming, close with two or three sentences that mention the topic of the paper. Then the reader will know when the paper is over, and all of our questions will be answered.

• Today we will be taking a look at endings and noticing how our endings can be improved.

❖ Part Two: Model.

Ms. Areglado models by showing the following piece on the overhead projector. Notice that the story's ending has a problem.

Last week I had a birthday party. Mom and Dad told me I could invite some friends to come, so I did. I asked three friends to come over. We played in the snow and made a snowman. We ate yummy chocolate birthday cake, then we ate ice cream, too. I was really excited when I opened my presents. I got safety equipment for my new bike. I got reflecting lights and a helmet. That's all.

Ms. Areglado: Can you put your finger under the ending and read it to me? How do you feel about the ending? Is it a smooth landing or a crash landing?

Justin: The ending came too quick. Our plane would have crashed!

Mrs. Miller: If it doesn't sound like it's over, what other questions do you have?

Ms. Areglado: Did the ending close up the topic?

Students: No.

Mrs. Miller: Did the ending convey feelings?

Students: No.

Ms. Areglado: Who has a suggestion for how this paper should end?

Brad: I think it should say something about how the person feels about the presents. Maybe he could say, "I got the equipment from by parents, and I will be sure I use all of it whenever I ride my bike." I also want to know how the kid feels about the party. He could say if he had fun at the birthday party.

Ms. Areglado: Excellent suggestions, Brad. You talked about feelings, and you referred to the topic of the paper, the birthday party.

Mrs. Miller: Boys and girls, try to end this practice paper by answering all of the questions you had about the ending.

Brad

The Birthday Party

Last week I had a birthday party. Mom and Dad told me I could invite some friends to come, so I did. I asked three friends to come over. ~~We played in the snow and made a snowman.~~ We ate my yummy chocolate birthday cake, then we ate ice cream, too. I was really excited when I opened my presents. I got safety equipment for my new bike, I got reflecting lights and a helmet. ~~That's all.~~ I relley like my birthday presents. They were relley nice toys. I was a litlle nervess and shy. The my freindms were aloud to sleep ove it was 10:00 when we went to bed. I had a good time with my friends at the birthday party.

Revisions of the ending completed in a cooperative group.

❖ **Part Three: Students Work in Cooperative Groups.**

Students work in groups as the teachers facilitate.

❖ **Part Four: Students From Each Group Share Their Revisions.**

As each cooperative group shares its endings, the teacher asks, "Did this ending answer your questions? Do you still want to know more?" Other students in the class vote as to whether the ending is complete.

❖ **Part Five: Each Student Revises His or Her Own Writing.**

If students seem ready for independent work, they take out a piece of their own writing and pay special attention to the ending.

Proofing *and* Editing Strategies

It is important to develop a criteria list with students on how to correct spelling errors and how to spell difficult words. Students use the lists as they write and when they proofread their work.

DEVELOPING A SPELLING CRITERIA LIST

In our school, teachers and children alike brainstorm the strategies they use to spell difficult words and to proofread their work. The teachers and children also demonstrate how to use the strategies, and then make lists like the following.

❖ **To spell difficult words I...**
- clap out the parts of the word as I say it aloud. Then I spell it in chunks.
- write the word with several different spellings to see which one looks correct.
- listen for the sounds in the word as I say it aloud.
- listen for chunks of the word that I know how to write.
- think if there is a familiar portion of the word I know.
- use the dictionary, Franklin Speller, Word Bank, or my personal dictionary.
- think about where I have seen the word before, and then I look it up.
- think about a common spelling rule I know. ("*i* before *e, except after c.*")
- think about the root word.
- think about how to write a word that sounds like the hard word.
- think about a clue I have been taught for words that sound alike but are spelled differently. ("The principal is my pal.")
- think about things I can draw to help me remember how to spell words. ("Two desserts for dessert"—to remember the two *ss*'s.)
- ask my neighbor.

❖ **To proofread for spelling mistakes I...**
- point to and read aloud what I have written.
- circle the words I think I misspelled.
- underline or write *sp* over the words I think I misspelled.
- use an extra piece of paper to uncover my writing, one line at a time, while I check my spelling.
- try again to spell correctly the words that I think I misspelled.

STRATEGIES TO IMPROVE EDITING FOR PUNCTUATION

We encourage our children to reread their pieces through all stages of the writing process, but particularly during the editing stage. We teach them useful strategies, such as:

- Read the piece aloud, pointing under each word. Look for errors. Make corrections.
- Check the beginning and end of each sentence to see if you remembered to put capitals and periods (or exclamation points).
- To check for commas, read the piece aloud, and determine when your voice naturally takes a rest. Place a comma there.

The editing checklists, like "My Grade One (Grade Two) Editing Checklist," are particularly helpful when they are developed interactively with the students.

TECHNIQUES FOR BUILDING CONFERRING SKILLS

Try these techniques for holding individual writing conferences with your primary children. Some of the ideas have been adapted from the work of Donald Graves.

- Listen to the student read his story to you.
- Comment on the content of the piece. Let the child know there is something special about the story. (Don't comment on mechanics now.) For example: "Tina, your mom will be so excited to read a book that is all about her. You did a great job of staying on-topic."
- Think about the content of the piece, and decide whether you want to refer to Graves's suggestions about revision. For example, if the piece is too brief, ask the student to provide more information.

Example: "Tina, I love the way you illustrated your mom on every page and wrote, 'My mom.' I can tell Mom is special to you. What kinds of things is Mom doing in this picture? Would you like to add that information on this page, so it will be clearer for the reader?

"Put your finger on the place where the new material should go. I can understand that section now, because you gave me more information."

Other Problems and Solutions:

- If the child comments that he wants to add information, but there is too much material for simply inserting it with a caret, teach the use of an asterisk. The child can find the place in the story that needs more information and write the asterisk in that spot on the draft. On a separate sheet of paper, the student places an asterisk and adds the new paragraph or section.

- If the child's piece rambles and lacks a central idea, ask, "If this piece is about _____, then why do we need material about _____?"

• If you cannot understand the piece, try another Graves technique. "I'm having trouble understanding what is happening here. Please explain what's going on."

•Examine the mechanics of the story during the writing conference, or set up a separate editing conference to do that.

• If the child's writing approaches standard spelling, ask, "Would you like me to show you how close you are to standard?" If the child agrees, print the standard spelling under the temporary spelling.

Lisa Holm confers with Kelly about her writing.

For example, if the child wrote *pensl,* say: "Your temporary spelling is very close to book spelling." Now, point to the child's writing, then point to your writing. "Look, you heard the *p,* the *e,* and the *n.* There is a tricky thing about the next letter. It sounds like an *s,* but really is a *c.* Sometimes *c* sounds like *s.* There is an *i* in-between the *s* and the *l.* Look, you heard the *l.* Good for you!"

• Fill out the following four assessment forms—which are modified from Donald Graves's ideas—with the student. (See appendix for reproducibles.) You can staple the sheets to the child's folder.

"Things _____ Can Do" Sheet
Ask the child what she did right about her writing. If she needs prompting, ask her to look at the class criteria list for effective writing. Working together with the student, make a list of the student's strengths. (You can also refer to the list when you fill out the child's report card.)

"Skills _____ Is Working On" Sheet
Set a "next step" for writing growth. Ask the child what skill or skills she'd like to work on, and write these down. (For example, "I need to learn how to punctuate the ends of sentences.")

"I Can Write About _____" Sheet
Check this sheet with the student. Update topic ideas, if necessary, by having the student draw and label ideas for future stories.

"Writing Completed By _____" Sheet
Ask the child to check this and update it.

• End the conference on a positive note. Recap for the child the specific things that were done well on the piece. Make sure that the child is proud of her accomplishments.

Tips for Avoiding Interruptions

- Choose an unusual accessory to wear as a sign that, unless there is an emergency, there should be no interruptions. For example, wear a yellow scarf to signal that you are busy.

- Develop a list of student experts with whom other students can consult.

- Make notepaper available. If a student is not satisfied with an answer from the student expert, he can write to you. Address the question after you and the conferee complete the session.

Ideas *for* Publishing Children's Work

Publishing is one of the best ways to celebrate children's writing. It is instantly rewarding and offers students a good deal of gratification. Here are some techniques that work well for us.

❖ **Author Celebrations—Parents Invited.** A popular program used by Nancy Areglado to recognize children's work includes:

- Parents are invited to school. We serve refreshments, which include one simple snack made by the students.
- Individual students receive their published books, along with a writing certificate of congratulations.
- Students read their published books to the parent or another adult.
- We present a slide show in which students are depicted participating in various phases of the writing process.

Catherine places her revised and edited kindergarten book into the publishing tub.

❖ **Writers' Club.** Students from the Writers' Club receive special certificates of accomplishment at the end of the year.

❖ **Signs.** Students whose work was published are recognized by the Parent/Teacher Association, who congratulate the students by writing their names and accomplishments on a huge school sign in front of the school.

❖ **On-the-Air.** Students who have published stories or poems are congratulated on-the-air over the daily Rolling Valley TV show, WRVS.

❖ **Authors' Awards.** All published authors receive awards at the end-of-the-year ceremonies. Students who submitted entries that were not published are congratulated and applauded. (See Appendix.) They are also asked to be guest speakers at one of the monthly Writers' Club meetings.

❖ **Displays.** Displaying students' writing in the classroom on bulletin boards and circulating copies through a classroom library gives a wonderful boost to young writers. A special section in the school library can be devoted to student works, so that children—across grade levels throughout the school—can borrow one anothers' published pieces.

A look of accomplishment is evident in Catherine and Jason as they admire their acrostic poems about penguins.

❖ **Displays Around Town.** Within the school's community, merchants and local libraries are delighted to showcase children's writing. Merchants are pleased to do this, especially since it often increases business.

❖ **Buddies Read Each Other's Books.** The classroom library of works written by the children can be used during D.E.A.R. (Drop Everything And Read) and can be extended to a checkout system for at-home reading. Students can take home their own books, and buddy editors can borrow the books, too.

❖ **Writers' Circle.** Both Mrs. Miller and Mrs. Holm make time to listen to what each student accomplished at the end of each writers' workshop. A child might say: "Today I finished meeting with my revision-and-editing buddy. I can see now I have to revise a little more. That is what I will do tomorrow, before my teacher conference." The teacher takes notes.

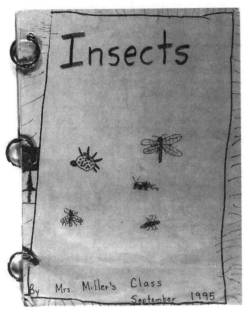

Mrs. Miller's class book on insects.

❖ **Class Books (Nonfiction).** Ask your children to each contribute a page to a class nonfiction book. This can be done at the end of a theme or as a response to a read-aloud. Each student writes a page. For example, Mrs. Miller asked the students to tell what they learned after listening to two books on bugs: *Insects and Crawly Creatures* and *A Child's Library of Learning—Insect World.*

❖ **Books Across the Miles.** Many of our students' grandparents live in other states. So we find ways to involve grandparents in celebrating their grandchildren's progress. We send published pieces, rather than commercially prepared cards, to grandparents on Grandparents' Day. This sends a strong message, both to the children and to the grandparents: "We value writing, we consider ourselves writers, and we are proud of our young writers' accomplishments." An added bonus is that grandparents are asked to write a response to their grandchildren. We also send students' pieces to aunts, uncles, cousins, other relatives, or close family friends.

❖ **Alphabet Books.** These can be written on a variety of subjects, and are often connected with a theme. Some teachers include alliterative elements in the alphabet books. For example, after a study of apples, a child might write on an *A* page: "appetizing apples."

Alphabet books can also become more expansive. For example, after a study of the presidents, the first page might say, "Abraham Lincoln, a great emancipator." Children may also write full sentences: "Abraham Lincoln was a great emancipator."

Melissa Miller taught grammar in conjunction with alphabet books. Her students made a class alphabet book on nouns, entitled *Nouns—Person, Place, Thing.*

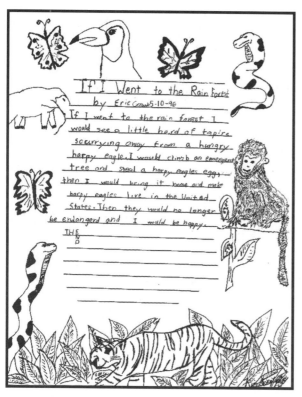

Eric's rain-forest story written on special bordered paper.

❖ **Special Borders.** Melissa Miller's students studied the endangered animals of the rain forest. The students wrote stories and developed them through the

After rain-forest pieces are published, the books decorate the classroom coatrack.

steps of the writing process. The unit culminated as Kimberly Areglado, Nancy's daughter, who is planning to become a primary teacher, designed a unique border for the students' final copies.

❖ **Flip Books.** Melissa Miller's students conducted research about the life of George Washington. The flip book they later made was a simple and concise way for students to share what they learned.

On each of five pages, students wrote facts about George Washington. They made illustrations to match the text, and decided on a sequential order that flowed well. They typed the text and edited on the computer. Final copies of the text were pasted inside each page of the book.

Mrs. Miller's class loves to publish flip books!

❖ **Class Poetry Books.** In Lisa Holm's class, students published a class poetry anthology. *The Best First Grade Poems Ever!* contains poems and illustrations composed by every student.

Justin puts the finishing touches on his tall-tale illustration.

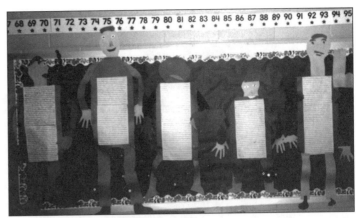

Mrs. Miller's class has illustrated and written stories about tall-tale people.

❖ **Life-Size Stories About Tall-Tale Heroes.** After reading a variety of tall tales and studying the genre, Melissa Miller's students wrote tall tales and illustrated them. Children's stories adorned the classroom.

❖ **Class Fiction Books.** Early in the year, Melissa Miller's second-grade students studied the genre of mysteries. The students wrote a class mystery together as a first story of the year. Each page was illustrated by groups of second graders.

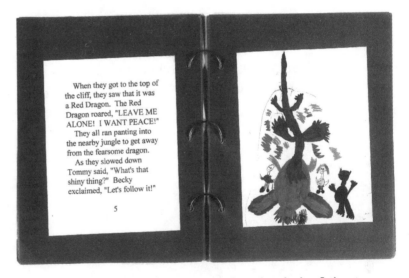

When they got to the top of the cliff, they saw that it was a Red Dragon. The Red Dragon roared, "LEAVE ME ALONE! I WANT PEACE!"

They all ran panting into the nearby jungle to get away from the fearsome dragon.

As they slowed down Tommy said, "What's that shiny thing?" Becky exclaimed, "Let's follow it!"

5

The Mystery of the Lost Pearl—early in the year. Second grade class fiction story.

A sample of Mrs. Miller's double-door book.

❖ **Double-Door Books.** Another popular book at Rolling Valley is the "double-door book." Students take a large rectangular piece of construction paper and fold it in fourths, with the right- and left-hand flaps shutting like double doors. Facts can be written on paper and pasted at the bottom of each of the four pages, and the top of each page can be illustrated. Once the "doors" are closed, they can be illustrated with the title of the project.

Brian shares his farm-shape book with Mrs. Godwin during sharing time in the kindergarten writers' workshop.

Josh decorates the cover of his dinosaur-shape book in his second-grade classroom.

❖ **Shape Books.** Children of all grades love to make shape books. These books can be designed to correspond with a theme. For example, if the class is studying wintertime weather, they can write stories in the shape of mittens. Kathy Godwin's class read *The Mitten* by Jan Brett, and then made a class shape book as a response.

Mitten-shape book from Mrs. Godwin's kindergarten.

❖ **Books About Events.** After students have gone on a field trip, they retell the trip as part of a language experience. Often, the teacher will be the scribe, writing as the children dictate.

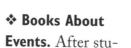

A language-experience book about a kindergarten trip to the apple barn.

Chapter Five

Helping Writers to Grow

Mrs. Miller confers with a student.

*I*n all classrooms there is a range of children's writing abilities. This chapter is devoted to sharing strategies that have been effective in assisting these children in developing and showing their writing talents.

❖ **Interactive Writing.** Interactive writing is a process in which the teacher—working one-on-one with a student—helps the child write a word or sentence in standard spelling. Often, the teacher shares the pen with the child. (Sharing the pen means that if the child does not know how to write a letter or a part of a word, the teacher would write it for him or her.) By spending just a few minutes a day, three times a week, on interactive writing, children make tremendous progress.

For example, first grader Samantha wrote: "I love dogs and cats." Samantha knew how to write *I*, but needed help with *love*. Mrs. Holm helped her to say the word and to hear the sounds. With *love* written correctly on her paper, Samantha continued to write the rest of the sentence, with some sharing of the pen with the teacher, until the whole sentence was complete.

❖ **Sentence Strips.** Sometimes we write sentences on strips and use them as puzzles for homework. For example, after the teacher helped Samantha to write her sentence in standard spelling, Samantha read her sentence as Mrs. Holm wrote it on a sentence strip. Then, Mrs. Holm cut up the same sentence into individual words. While Samantha was reassembling the sentence, Mrs. Holm wrote the sentence on the front of a legal-size envelope. They put the words in the envelope. Now, Samantha had a sentence puzzle to take home. The teacher added a note to parents about the activity.

❖ **Letter Formation Help.** The art of writing is exciting for most students, but for those who have difficulty forming letters, writing is frustrating. We assess which letters are difficult for a child to make. Once the child learns that letter, we make sure the next letter the child learns is formed with similar strokes. For example, if a child has learned to write o, she would then learn to write *p*, because it, too, is formed from a round shape.

❖ **Making Books.** Are there students in your class who don't make progress in writing because there are many words they can't write? Making Books is a tutoring program that was designed by Nancy Areglado for volunteers who work with emergent writers. It is a modified version of the book-making suggestions of Marie Clay in *Becoming Literate*.

Classroom teachers select Making Books candidates by asking emergent writers, during a ten-minute period, to list all of the words they know how to write. Teachers use prompts, such as, "Write the names of people in your family, your best friends, your relatives."

For each student, the teacher simply lists the "known words" that the child can write in standard spelling. This provides the parent or volunteer with a base. Then she makes a book with the child that celebrates those words. If a child needs help, the teacher "shares the pen" with the child.

Kimberly Areglado is a Making Books volunteer. Kimberly looks at P.J.'s list of known words. She notices P.J. knows how to write *love* and *P.J.* Kimberly asks P.J. to choose some stickers that show objects that he loves. He places them in a book. They continue with other words, all the while reinforcing what the child knows. They create highly predictable text that matches each sticker.

Kimberly Areglado and P.J. are ready to use the Making Books box.

Using the Appeal of Rhyme

"My first-grade students study a new poem each week. One activity children enjoy is to identify rhyming words within the poem. Sometimes, we look at a group of rhyming words, decide what family the words belong to, and brainstorm other words that belong with them.

"For example, the class identified *away, day,* and *play* as rhyming words in the poem 'It's Spring' by Winifred J. Mott. (It's important to teach word families within a context of meaningful reading, such as a poem, chant, or story.) During the next few minutes, students produce these "relatives": *may, way, stay, today, Kay, say, nay, Jay, pray, OK, lay, clay,* and *pay.* Later in the day, I write the 'family' name and family members on one of our word-family houses.

"If students are perplexed about how to write a word, I prompt them with this question: 'Do you know a word that sounds like that? Can you write it?'"

— Lisa Holm

❖ **Shared Writing.** This is a procedure in which the teacher writes on the board a story or sentence that she and the class write together. As the teacher thinks aloud, students see how writing in standard spelling works. ("Let's see. I'm writing someone's name. So I'll use a capital letter.") Students make links between sounds and symbols, learn spacing, learn "known words" they can write, and learn to write chunks of words, such as *-ing* endings.

❖ **Morning Message.** A great way to start off the day, the Morning Message tells about an event that will happen that day. ("Today we will go on a trip to the zoo.") The children dictate the message while the teacher writes at the board. Many teachers use Shared Writing with their Morning Message. As the teacher introduces Morning Message, she thinks aloud at the end of each sentence. For example, she may say, "I'll write the next word below this line of print, way over here on the left. That's what we do when we write."

Lessons on grammar, punctuation, spacing

Joel finishes the last correction on the Morning Message, which focuses on content integration and the cloze strategy.

between words, and capitalization can all be built into the think-aloud. For example, the teacher can say, "Today we is going to........Oh!......I mean today we *are* going to have an assembly. If I say 'is going,' it just won't sound right."

After the teacher and children figure out how to write that line of print, she may ask, "How should we end the sentence, girls and boys? Are we telling or asking when we say, 'Today we are going to have an assembly?"

Punctuation is a natural for Morning Message lessons—children become familiar with commas, quotation marks, and, especially, exclamation points.

TEACHER TIP

Kinesthetic Punctuation

Each morning we begin our day by sharing news through the Morning Message. After composing the message and fixing any parts we feel need attention, our V.I.P. (Very Important Person) leads the class in reading the message aloud. Adding kinesthetic punctuation provides a terrific reinforcement of capitalization and punctuation skills for all the children, especially those who learn best through movement.

I introduce kinesthetic punctuation early in the year, when we are working on starting each sentence with a capital letter and ending with a stop sign (a period). I explain to the class that we are going to read our message using movements for capital letters and stop signs. The class then decides what movements to use. We begin with the following: capital letters—hands and arms extend above our heads; periods—right hand extends (palm facing out) in front of the chest; exclamation points—jump straight up and down; question marks—scratch the chin with the right hand while creating a questioning look.

Students raise their arms to display capital letters during Kinesthetic Punctuation time in Mrs. Holm's first-grade room.

After reviewing the Morning Message, we stand and read it again, incorporating each movement in the appropriate place. The children love this energetic reading!

Throughout the year, our repertoire expands as we become more sophisticated writers. Eventually we add motions for the apostrophe, parentheses, caret, and degree symbol. Engaging the class in this active learning definitely makes the Morning Message come alive.

—Lisa Holm

FOCUS LESSON: HELPING STUDENTS WHO ARE STUCK ON THE FIRST SENTENCE

Kelsey finishes her final copy of leads, while Andrew works on his portfolio folder.

Colleen Connally completed her student teaching in Melissa Miller's second-grade class. Through her assessment of the children during writers' workshop, Colleen noticed that some had difficulty getting started writing, even though they had already chosen their topic. They just didn't know how to begin the first sentence. Here's a lesson for helping them.

1. Read students the picture book, *The Umbrella*.
2. As a response to the book, ask children to list some of their favorite things.
3. Have them take three ideas and write three different leads. Revise the leads.
4. Publish students' final copies (leads only) by writing them on paper raindrops, which are suspended with yarn from paper umbrellas. This is in keeping with the theme of *The Umbrella*.

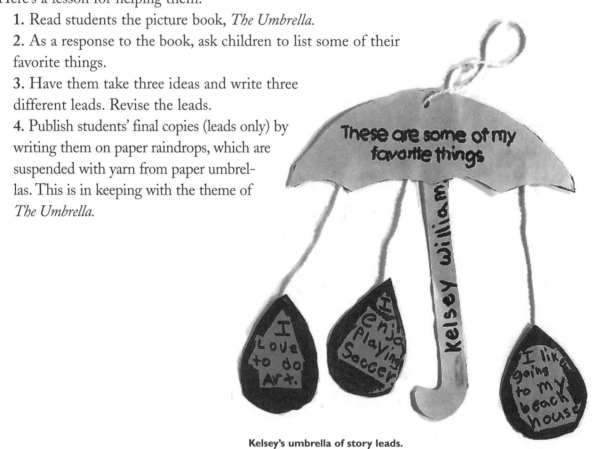

Kelsey's umbrella of story leads.

Chapter Six

The Benefits *of* Writing Across *the* Curriculum

Nate and Brian read the big book their class wrote about the barn trip.

*H*ave you discovered the benefit of integrating writing across the curriculum? At Rolling Valley, integration is our teachers' key to accomplishing much within the short school day. Integration is possible because, by using large blocks of time devoted to one project, we address several subjects at once.

Our students in kindergarten, grade one, and grade two use their knowledge of writers' workshop to great advantage. They apply the writing-process techniques to their writing in science, math, and social studies, and often bring content-area pieces to final copy at workshop time.

78

INTEGRATING WRITING IN MATH

Lisa Holm combines a number of effective strategies in a single lesson. For example, she may model for her first graders revision strategies for math writing, and also develop criteria with them for writing a book on a math topic. In the following example, Lisa starts by writing a sentence on the board, then thinks her revision technique aloud.

"At 5:30 A.M., my alarm wakes me up," Holm writes on her draft. Holm rereads her work, commenting that it would be more specific if she said, "I get up at 5:30 A.M. and make breakfast." She continues drafting and revising. Later, she invites her students to write stories of their own. But she guides them to set up criteria for their books on the subject.

Our criteria for time books:
- Tell how time affects your day.
- Tell what happens in the morning, afternoon, and evening.
- Make the time on the clock for each description.
- Make pictures that match each description.

The children finish the project by writing out their stories in the form of flip books.

WRITING IN SOCIAL STUDIES: MELISSA MILLER

"My second graders have been enthusiastically publishing their work in a variety of ways—typing on bordered paper, printing in pr-made books of various colors, and making shape books. As the class nears the end of their unit on George Washington, I tell them that they will soon be publishing a book about Washington in a special and new way. I hear Mandy whisper to her neighbor, 'I can't wait to publish my book!'

"The next day, after reviewing facts, I ask students to write five interesting sentences about George Washington. We review the writing process, and I remind them that the piece will go to final copy. As the children finish their drafts, they meet with a buddy to revise and edit, then confer with me to prepare for publishing.

"Throughout the day, each child types his five facts. When it's time to publish, I present the new format—a flip book. Amid cries of 'Oh! I like that!' and 'That's a good idea!' I give directions. Each child will cut out the typed sentences and glue one sentence on each page of the book. Then, the book is ready for illustrations.

"The final products bring cheers as they are

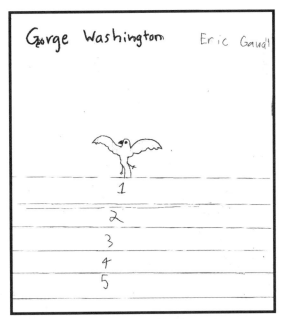

Eric's flip book about George Washington has been brought to final copy. It demonstrates writing across the curriculum.

shared in the Author's Chair. Students vote to place the published books in the class reading center. Edges of the books soon become worn from frequent reading, which shows that non-fiction writing is popular in my class."

Response Logs

With Response Logs, students explain —through words or pictures—what they learned.

LEARNING LOGS

With learning logs, children respond in areas across the curriculum. At Rolling Valley, learning logs are used throughout the school in every grade, even kindergarten. They encourage learning in math, science, and social studies, because they help students link prior knowledge with new information.

In addition, learning logs identify misconceptions and provide immediate feedback to the teacher on what was understood in the unit. Because of this feedback, learning logs aid teachers in planning future lessons. All children, no matter what their abilities, can be included in and successful at using learning logs.

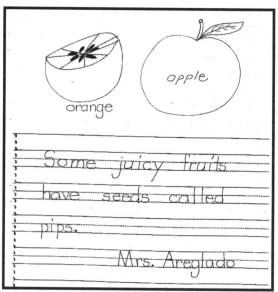

❖ **Class Learning-Log Books**

An easy way to introduce students to learning logs is to make a class learning-log book and connect it to a theme.

For example, Nancy Areglado had students in Mrs. Holm's first-grade class create a class book on plants. Before students wrote in their individual logs, she modeled for students guidelines for writing, storing, and submitting entries.

Teacher modeling format of a class learning-log entry.

❖ **General Guidelines**

• **Topic**—Select a theme, such as Plants.

• **When to Write**—Set aside a time for your students to write in the class learning log.

• **Format of Entry**—Decide how the entry should look. Model a sample entry, writing it on the first page. (See sample, right.)

• **Location**—Decide where the log(s) will be located. (It's usually in the learning center of the theme being studied.)

• **Completion Date**—Announce the date by which the writing should be completed.

Students make self-portraits of themselves as president.

❖ **Establish Log's Format**

It's important to develop criteria with the students for the format of the learning-log entry. For example, every grading quarter, kindergarten teacher Kathy Godwin staples together blank sheets for the learning-log booklets for each child. Her format is as follows: Students are to draw a picture of what they learned on the top part of the sheet and write what they learned at the bottom of a sheet.

Formats can vary. Some teachers connect learning logs to a theme. For example, when Nancy Areglado taught a social studies theme about the presidents, she invited students to depict themselves as the president during the year 2028 and to draw self-portraits on the cover of their learning-log books.

❖ **Show sample responses.**

Showing examples of responses is vital to getting quality learning-log responses from students. Often, teachers will show two mock samples. As students look at each response and compare them, it is easy for them to notice differences. Then the class develops criteria for writing a good learning-log entry.

Second-Grade Samples
Theme: Dairy Products

Dear Mrs. Miller,
    I lerned that ice cream is in the milk famlee.
    Jamie

SAMPLE 1

September 12, 1996
    Dear Mrs. Miller,
    I learned that I can make butter by shaking up cream in a bottle. Now, I know that butter and cream are in the milk group. I also learned that I eat a lot of dairy foods. I drink milk and sometimes Mom bys me frozen yogert. I love ice cream. It's my favorit dairy product. I learned that cottag cheese is also a dairy food.
    Your student,
    Catherine

SAMPLE 2

❖ Compare Samples, Develop Criteria

When developing criteria for learning logs, the teacher asks students to compare Sample One with Sample Two. "Boys and girls, could you please read these learning-log samples aloud and tell three things you notice about the differences between them?"

The students brainstorm answers and prove their points by pointing to the text. For example, Joshua proved that Sample One contained more details. His teacher helped him to rephrase this as, "Tell details about what you learned," and placed this statement on the criteria chart. The lesson continued in cooperative groups, and a criteria chart was the result.

> Our criteria for learning logs:
> 1. Write today's date on the right side of your log sheet.
> 2. Make your learning log sheet like a letter to your teacher.
> 3. Tell details about what you learned.
> 4. Tell how you feel about what you learned.

❖ Model a Variety of Learning-Log Techniques

During the first quarter of the school year, a great deal of teacher modeling takes place, because students are learning routines for how to respond in the log. Later, children have a wide repertoire from which to choose. We teach our children these techniques:

• Make a K - W - L chart on a theme being studied.
K = What I Know; W = What I Want to Know; L = What I Learned.
• Complete a science experiment sheet. Staple it to the log. (See Appendix.)
• Summarize a new concept that you learned.
• Define math terms, such as *geometric shapes*, or explain science vocabulary words, such as *pupa*.
• Tell feelings, questions, or confusions about what you studied.
• Pretend to explain to a young student a new idea that you learned. Be specific.
• Research a topic, and write about what you learned.
• Tell about new ideas you discovered on your own.
• Write a letter to the teacher explaining what it is that you do not understand.
• Draw pictures that help you remember important things. Write explanations beside them.

MATH ENTRIES IN THE LEARNING LOG

Tom Wrightman, a math expert from Oregon, found that his students enjoyed responding about math so much that they each wanted a math log of their own.

Here are some ideas for what children can write in their logs:

• **Explanations for Procedures.** Explain a procedure, such as how to carry a numeral in addition, or define a math term, such as *rectangle*.

- **Real Story Problems.** Write real story problems with data collected in the classroom or school. For example, students collect data about shoes and graph the information. Later they write a narrative telling the kinds of shoes that are most popular in class.
- **Equations.** Children write a story that fits an equation, such as 2 + 3 = 5.
- **Number Clues.** Select a numeral, and write sentences that describe it. The writer reads one of his number clues to a partner. The partner guesses the number. If it is incorrect, another clue is read.
- **Goof Reviews.** After a child makes a mistake on a problem or an equation, he corrects it by explaining how to fix it.
- **Graphing Narrative.** Write an explanation for a bar graph or another type of graph. Attach the graph to the explanation.
- **Solving a Problem.** Write details that help in solving a particular problem.
- **Manipulative Predictions.** Analyze uncertain situations or problems by using manipulatives to solve outcomes. The predictions are written in sentences.
- **Rhyming Numbers.** Select a number and create a rhyme for it. This number is illustrated by a picture.
- **Math Happening.** Write how math is part of everyday life. (Lisa Holm has developed this concept with her class. Their math problem was to count the total number of spots on the ladybugs. Their answer appears at the bottom of the sample, upside-down.)

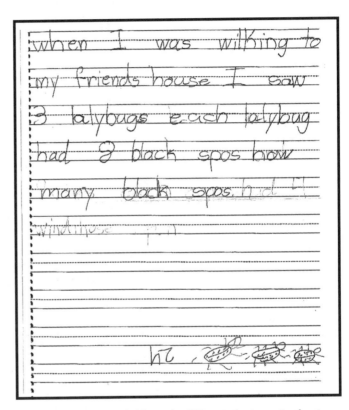

An example of a "Math Happening." Two students wrote about walking to a friend's house and noticing ladybugs along the way.

SCIENCE ENTRIES IN THE LEARNING LOG

Science entries in the learning log are usually connected with the theme that the students are studying. Often teachers like to have individual student logs just for that particular theme, such as the farm (see next page). However, it is certainly appropriate to have one general learning-log book with entries on science as well as other subjects. Science responses can reflect the scientific processes of observing, predicting, analyzing, discovering, and drawing conclusions.

Data collection is another purpose of the science log. See samples below.

Kindergarten students make a farm log book after their field trip.

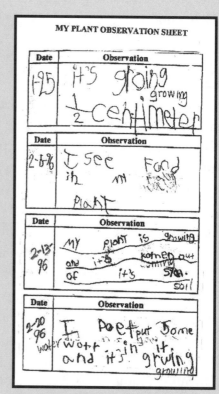

Michael's science data collection sheet reflects the scientific processes.

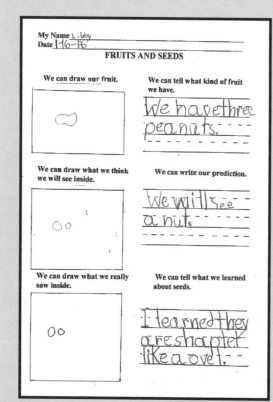

Libby's prediction sheet helps her get personally involved with science.

Michael observes and draws conclusions in his learning-log entry.

Sometimes science entries explain a process that the students understand, such as in the kindergarten sample shown here. Two students understand the growth process that amphibians go through in becoming frogs and also that pupas go through in becoming butterflies.

The students tell how butterflies are born.

❖ **Science-log entries can compare and contrast.**

They can also be used for comparison and contrast, as is displayed in the sample, right.

Diagrams help students compare and contrast information.

Grade-two students summarize facts they learned about Dr. Martin Luther King, Jr.

SOCIAL-STUDIES LEARNING LOGS

Students can incorporate into their social-studies logs the same type of responses as in science and math logs. Graphic organizers can be stapled or written into the learning log. The Venn diagram, above, was written directly into the log.

READING LOGS

Regie Routman, in her book *Invitations*, defined a literature-response log as a means for recording reactions to literature. The log helps students connect reading to writing, extends the meaning of the text, promotes critical thinking, and helps readers become more personally involved with the book. Responses in the log go far beyond merely summarizing and recalling facts. All types of graphic organizers connected with literature, such as story maps or Venn diagrams, can easily be placed into the reading log.

❖ Help students interact with literature with reading logs.

Reading logs are used occasionally with students in kindergarten, and routinely with students in grades one and higher. As with learning logs, the teacher spends a great deal of time modeling how to respond. When used in kindergarten, the teacher shows how to respond to literature in a simple way.

The teacher shows how to respond in the reading log in the same way she models how to respond in the learning log. She demonstrates how to write a log response, and the students develop criteria for their own writing, based on what they observed. The teacher shows two samples: one well-written, the other poorly written, that reflect the writing of her students. She has the class point out differences between the two.

Here are two such samples, created by Nancy Areglado, followed by the criteria charts that second-grade children made about reading-log entries.

Reading Log Samples

Dear Mrs Milr,
I red a funny book. I liked it a lot. It made me laf. It was about six litl pigs. Maybe you mite like to read it sometime. I think you wod like it to.
Marion

SAMPLE 1

SAMPLE 2

September 22, 1996
Dear Mrs. Miller,
I read a book called The Great Pig Escap. It was written by Eileen Christelow. When I think about this book, all I can do is laugh and laugh. It was fiction and it was very funny! It's about a man namd Bert and a lady namd Ethel. They bot six little piglets. Thes piglets were vry smart! They didn't want to be made into pork chops. The funny part was how they escaped from the truck on the way to the auction. They dressd up in people's clothes. It's amazing to me how no one regnised them. How could they not notice those big, big snouts? Boy, that book sure was funny!
Your student,
Steven

SECOND-GRADE CRITERIA FOR READING LOGS

❖ **Early in the Year (after teacher models each one)**:
  - Write the date.
  - Write a letter to Mrs. Miller about the book.
  - Tell the title.
  - Tell the author.
  - Tell your feelings about the book.
  - Tell details about the book.
  - Tell about the characters in the book.

❖ **End of the Year (after teacher models each one)**:
  - Write the date.
  - Write a letter to Mrs. Miller about the book.
  - Tell the title.
  - Tell the author.
  - Tell your feelings about the book.
  - Tell details about the book.
  - Tell about the characters in the book.
  - Tell about the setting in the book.
  - Make predictions about what will happen.
  - Tell if your predictions came true.
  - Make a Venn diagram comparing characters or comparing books.
  - Tell your favorite part of the book and why you liked it.
  - Retell the book with pictures and sentences.
  - Compare yourself to a character in the book.
  - Write a different ending to the book.
  - Do a story map on the book.
  - Pretend you are a character, and write a letter to another character in the book.
  - Tell why you think the author wrote the book.
  - Make a story web telling the title and author in the middle of the web, and telling the beginning, middle, end, problem, and solution on the surrounding spokes of the web.
  - Draw and tell the beginning, middle, end, problem, and solution.
  - Draw your favorite character. Make a character bubble telling something that your character might say.
  - Rate your book on a scale of zero to ten and tell why.

TYPES OF READING-LOG RESPONSES

Here are some ways children can respond in their reading logs:

Libby works on her draft for Mrs. Holm's class version of *The Important Book.*

❖ **Written Retelling.** Written retelling is a way to tell whether the child understood what was read.

❖ **Compare Characters.** Sometimes children compare events in the characters' lives to similar events in their own lives.

OTHER TYPES OF RESPONSES TO LITERATURE

Here are additional ways to help children respond to the books they've read.

❖ **Class Books.** In Lisa Holm's first-grade class, the students read Margaret Wise Brown's classic, *The Important Book.* Lisa then modeled what she feels is important to her. Her students brainstormed ideas of what is important to them and prepared drafts on special response paper. They went through the steps of the writing process, and the final copies were entered into the computer.

> Alex 6-13-96
>
> The important thing about my Dog is that my Dog is big. I can hug my Dog. He is very fat. He's very fluffy.
> But the important thing about my Dog is that my Dog is big.
>
> Alex, you used big as the important thing about your dog. What else can you say about your dog?

> The important thing about my dog is my dog is big. I can hug my dog. He is very fat. He's very fluffy. But the important thing about my dog is that my dog is big.
>
> Alex Witt

Alex's "important thing" draft and final copy shows his revising and editing skills.

❖ **Extensions to Books.** In Kathy Godwin's kindergarten classroom, students studied weather and space, and day and night. Kathy read *Sun up, Sun down*, written by Gail Gibbons. Students wrote responses about what they like to do in the daytime and at night. Their responses were accompanied by drawings and were placed in a class big book.

Amber and Katie read the kindergarten version of *Sun up, Sun down*.

Brook's response to the book *Sun up, Sun down*, makes the book more personal to her.

The children in kindergarten were studying weather, and they discussed different kinds of wind, from a breeze to a gust. The teacher read aloud *The Wind Blew* by Pat Hutchins. In addition to art projects on the subject, the children wrote a big book called *The Wind Blew*.

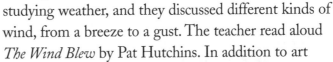

❖ **Writing Predictions.** When Lisa Holm's class started studying the genre of fairy tales, each child responded with what he or she might expect to see in a fairy tale, based on his or her own prior knowledge.

Nate and Arielle show the class big book *The Wind Blew*.

Kasey and Chris display projects they made as they wrote fairy tale predictions.

❖ **Writing New Endings.** As part of their plant study, the students in Mrs. Godwin's kindergarten read the big book of *Jack and the Beanstalk*. As a response to the story, they made pictures of Jack and the beanstalk and rewrote the ending.

Mrs. Godwin's students loved reading Bill Martin, Jr.'s famous book, *Brown Bear, Brown Bear, What Do You See?* Once students were familiar with the repetitive pattern of the text, they wrote an extension to another of his books, *Polar Bear, Polar Bear, What Do You See?*

Joey, Giovanna, and Joshua show their *Jack and the Beanstalk* extensions.

Students illustrated each page by applying crayons to construction paper, then washed the entire picture with white paint.

Kindergarten extension to Bill Martin, Jr.'s *Polar Bear, Polar Bear, What Do You See?*

WRITING IN DIFFERENT GENRES

❖ **Journal Writing.** By writing in a journal, children connect writing to events that happened to them in school and at home.

• When the teacher models journal writing, her primary purpose is to show that journal writing makes sense.

• Journals are not usually edited, but if a piece is going to be taken to final copy, the journal may be. Often, when the children write in temporary spelling, teachers will write in standard spelling (below the temporary spelling) because the children's spelling is so emergent. However, this is not a correction.

❖ **Sample Areas for Journal Writing.**

• **Feelings.** The child can tell her emotional reaction to events, such as her feelings about a birthday party.

• **Sharing Lives.** The child can describe an event in his life. For example, he may write that his friend's mom is expecting a baby.

• **Hopes.** A student may tell about her plans for the future ("When I grow up, I'll _____.") and

Colin reads his kindergarten journal to Mrs. Godwin.

add an illustration.

• **Feelings About School.** A child may write about an exciting school event, such as a chick hatching.

• **Imagining.** A child can tell about his fantasies, such as imagining what would happen if a dinosaur entered the classrom.

❖ **Dialogue Journals.** Early in the year, Nancy Areglado introduced dialogue journals to a first-grade class. Students were happy to receive responses or "mail" on a daily basis from the teacher! Often they would crowd around one another's entries to see what their friends' notes said (see sample, below).

After months of dialoguing, the students started losing interest. So Areglado wrote a funny response to one child. All the other students asked Areglado to write funny responses in their journals, too. For the rest of the year, enthusiasm for journals was strong. Sometimes, the children laughed before they even got to the section that was humorous!

Children enjoy responding to the teacher in their dialogue journals.

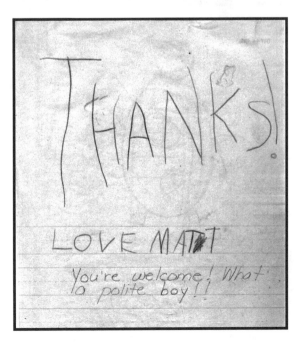

Q&A Morning Message

I introduced the Question-and-Answer Morning Message to acquaint my morning and afternoon classes with each other. Each day, the morning class answers a question posed the previous day by the afternoon class. Then, the morning class asks a question of the afternoon class. That afternoon, the afternoon class answers the question, then asks one of its own. For example:

Angelica prepares a message for her pen pal.

> P.M. class: How many kids are there in your class?
>
> A.M. class: There are 28 kids in our class.
>
> A.M. class: What is your favorite color?
>
> P.M. class: Our favorite color is red.

This served as one means of teaching the difference between a statement, or "telling sentence," and a question, or "asking sentence."

As an extension, I created a Pen Pal Message Center. In this center, the children can send a message (telling or asking) to a student in the other class. The children wrote messages during circle time or as an independent activity when assigned tasks were completed. The children's individual cubbies serve as mailboxes, and the prepared forms provide a format for their messages.

—Kathy Godwin

KINDERGARTEN MESSAGE SHEET

To My Penpal, Kelly,

DOYOU Like PeZZA?

From Arielle

Arielle asks Kelly, a student in the P.M. kindergarten class, a question in her message.

KINDERGARTEN MESSAGE SHEET

To My Penpal, Arielle,

Yes I ll ke PiSSA

From Kelly

Kelly, a P.M. kindergarten student, answers Arielle's question.

Message Center

Introducing a message center encouraged my students to pursue a new form of nonfiction writing. Interest was sparked when the children discovered a bank of mailboxes, individually labeled with classmates' names.

During writers' workshop, we defined a message as "a short piece of writing to another person, which tells something or asks a question, or both." We then brainstormed a list of people to whom we might write messages, as well as a list of ideas for message contents. Next, we developed a format, discussing the need to identify both the sender and the receiver.

One morning, I asked the children to write a message to a classmate. After lunch, the children were thoroughly delighted as they checked their mailboxes and read their messages. All the children, especially those who had been asked questions, were eager to write replies.

I keep the Message Center well-stocked with a variety of notepaper, and I participate as a writer. This has helped the children maintain a keen interest in this writing form."

—Lisa Holm

Alex places a message in a classmate's message can.

Alex and Kelly read the messages they received.

Integrating Poetry Across *the* Curriculum

Integrating poetry into subject areas across the curriculum is a great timesaver and motivator. For example, for Earth Day, Colleen Connally taught second graders how to write a cinquain about water.

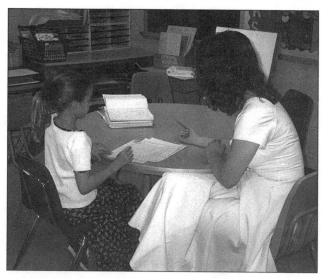

Mrs. Miller meets with Kelsey to revise and edit her poem.

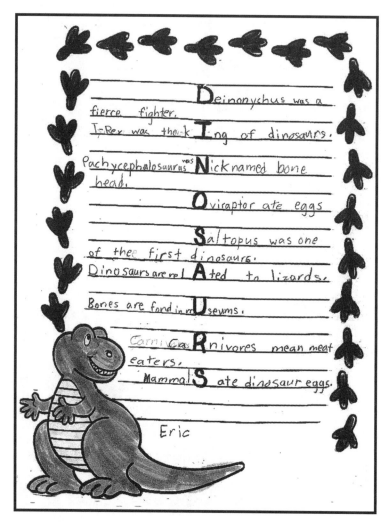

Eric's dinosaur acrostic poem shows his understanding of facts about dinosaurs.

ACROSTICS

Acrostics are widely used by teachers as a summary activity when a theme is finished. Colleen Connally and Melissa Miller worked with second-grade students to create this acrostic on dinosaurs. The teachers wrote the word *dinosaur* on the chalkboard vertically, and then brainstormed possible statements from facts learned about the subject. Each child then wrote his or her own poem.

Sandra and Michael display wind socks and poems about the wind.

Free verse written by Kasey during theme on weather. Illustrated on a wind sock.

Name Kelsey Williams
Line 1: Name of hero

Line 2: 3 verbs ending in ing

Lines 3
      4   3 phrases telling where
      5   he might be found

Line 6: One sentence about Paul

Line 1: Paul P. Bunyan

Line 2: baking, growing, floating,

Line 3: In near Alaska

Line 4: In the woods

Line 5: all around the world

Line 6: The biggest man on Earth!

Kelsey's tall-tale planning page. She will illustrate it on an art sample of Paul Bunyan's ax.

WIND-SOCK POETRY

Linking poetry with art and science was easy for Kasey Lovett, a first-grade student who wrote a poem about the wind and displayed it on a wind sock. The verse was written during a study about weather.

TALL-TALE POEMS

Poetry and literature were linked in the study of Paul Bunyan, when second-grade students in Melissa Miller's classroom wrote tall-tale poems in conjunction with the study of the genre.

Chapter Seven

Assessing Your Students' Writing

Assessment drives instruction. This one statement is perhaps the most fundamental idea to understand about assessment. Know this is true for your teaching, and you're way ahead of the game!

Here, watch the interplay between teaching and assessment:

Ms. Areglado: Delante, I noticed you added an apostrophe in your piece. I'm impressed that you've started to use apostrophes.
Delante: I learned how to use them from the Morning Message. The story said, "Today is Justin's birthday."

Initially, Delante placed the apostrophe in the wrong place in his story. Ms. Areglado praised Delante for using it at all, though, and noted on his anecdotal record form that he needs more help in that area.

Later that day, in writers' workshop, Ms. Areglado asked Delante to help her by modeling where to add the apostrophes in a short paragraph, which was on the overhead projector.

Delante proudly filled in the apostrophes in the correct places. The lesson ended. As the students began their writers' workshop—with some students drafting, revising, editing, publishing, and meeting with peers—Ms. Areglado quickly jotted a comment in Delante's anecdotal record, noting that he was now able to add apostrophes on his own. Then, after making sure that everyone was on task, she began her teacher/student conferences.

This is an example of how routine assessment drives a teacher's instruction. Ms. Areglado observed that Delante was attempting to use apostrophes and realized he was ready for more instruction in that skill. The anecdotal notes Ms. Areglado took on Delante's progress were brief, but became her record of his progress for that day:

> Delante - 10/20
>
> ~Used an apostrophe incorrectly the first time he wrote in his journal: "Today is Justins' birthday."
>
> ~Modeled correctly five times in a focus lesson on apostrophes where the apostrophe should be placed.

In her notes (whether on a class anecdotal list or an individual comment sheet), Ms. Areglado often includes examples from the student's writing, thus illustrating her point.

CLASS ANECDOTAL RECORD

Our teachers often keep class anecdotal forms in the front section of a loose-leaf binder, which is devoted to assessment. Each tab in the front section represents a subject: writing, social studies, geography, science, math, reading, and health. Students' names are listed down the left-hand side, in alphabetical order. It's easy to locate the same student's name from subject heading to subject heading, because these names always appear in the same place.

Often, at the close of writers' workshop, the teacher uses a class anecdotal sheet to record each student's progress. She quickly writes down what each student covered in the workshop that day, and jots down what will be covered the following day.

Samples
Topic: What Was Covered in Writing Workshop

Aaron 4/16/96

Today - revised and edited with a buddy. Fixed his work.

Tomorrow - will be in a teacher/student conference.

Alyssa 4/16/96

Today - used carets in writing and dictionaries to revise.

Tomorrow - will revise and edit with a buddy.

OTHER USES

Class sheets can also be used for other purposes. For example, if a teacher is assessing how well kindergarten students drew and labeled a story idea, the anecdotal record may look like this:

Josephine 11/12/96

Writing matched the picture; made sense; consonant spelling used.
"M D pl w me."
My dad plays with me.

Joshua 11/12/96

Writing in circular scribbles; oral retelling of what scribbles mean - very clear; scribbles match the picture.

It is important to date each entry and copy a sentence or two directly from the student's writing. This gives the teacher vital information about the child's progress in spelling and phonics. The more specific the teacher's comments about the sample, the more informative and useful the entry.

The sample, right, depicts children in grade one who wrote about what they learned in social studies about George Washington. Nancy Areglado wrote anecdotal comments.

MANAGEMENT ROUTINES

Teachers sometimes develop a schedule on which they list who will be evaluated each day. Often, teachers carry a clipboard with the "Class Anecdotal Record" sheet attached. Then they take notes on two or more students per day. We recommend you try this, too.

For example, if your class has 28 students and you make a progress report for two children daily, you'd complete your class anecdotals in 14 days. Then, the cycle of assessment begins again. In addition, you may write observations about students (like Delante) who did something that was unusual.

Class anecdotal record form—social studies—lets you see how the whole class is doing.

❖ **Skills to Assess.**

You may take notes on any of the following skills:
- Used directionality.
- Used correct spacing.
- Made sense.
- Wrote in sentences.
- Included a beginning, middle, end, and problem and/or solution.
- Included paragraphs.
- Used details.
- Had an interesting lead.
- Stayed on topic.
- Concluded with a strong ending.
- Knows letter sounds.

Class anecdotal assessment form—writing. Class anecdotal forms help the teacher see where the class and individuals are in writing development.

You can use the "Developmental Stages of Writing—Individual Checklist" to assess the progress of each child (see Appendix). You can review both the class list and the individual list to find topics for upcoming lessons that match skill needs.

During her teacher/student writing conference, Lisa Holm took notes on an anecdotal class list (see left).

USING THE ANECDOTAL RECORD TO TEACH A FOCUS LESSON

❖ **Staying On-Topic.**
Mrs. Miller's anecdotal records showed that some of her students wrote stories that were off-topic. She asked Nancy Areglado to use "writing on-topic" as the subject of her lesson. She brought in a poster of a movable airplane, which she would use in the lesson. Then Nancy modeled how to revise the following story.

Sandi and the Enormous Brown Bear

Sandi just couldn't believe it! She wondered if what she saw, or thought she saw, could really be true. As she skipped along her street, an enormous brown bear came walking towards her. "Good day, Sandi," said the bear as it smiled at her. Now, Sandi's parents had taught her not to talk to strangers. Sandi's mom reminded her about when her sister was lost, every time Sandi left the house.

"Remember when Stephanie was lost in the grocery store?" Mom would say, "She was only lost for five minutes. She knew what to do, because she saw a policeman. He found me shopping in the store and brought her to me and talked to her about how important it is to stay with her mom in the store."

Every time I left the house, all I could think of was that story about Stephanie in the grocery store. Even though my sister always got into trouble, I was glad she was all right.

Ms. Areglado: What is the title?

Students: "Sandi and the Enormous Brown Bear."

Ms. Areglado: What do you expect the story to be about?

Maria: Someone named Sandi and a big, giant bear.

Ms. Areglado: That makes sense. Let's read it and see.

As the students read the story aloud, they realized it was off-topic. Now Ms. Areglado showed them the poster of the movable airplane. They discussed how a plane takes off, stays on-course, and comes in for a smooth landing.

Ms. Areglado: There is another way our writing is just like an airplane trip. The pilot tells where we are going. What does the captain on the plane do? He stays on-course, and that's like us staying on-topic when we write. Did the story "Sandi and the Enormous Brown Bear" stay on-topic?

Sonya: No! It only talked about the bear saying hello. We never found out what happened after that to Sandi and the bear.

Ms. Areglado: You are correct, Sonya. What other questions or comments do you have?

Will: The part about Sandi's sister and the policeman just doesn't fit.

The children continued brainstorming with Ms. Areglado. In their cooperative groups, they worked on revising the sample, and they shared more revisions. At the end of the lesson, they revised a second piece. Later, they reviewed their own pieces of writing to see if they were on-topic.

Writing Assessment Throughout *the* Year

BEGINNING OF THE YEAR

Teachers at Rolling Valley use several activities to assess their students at the start of the school year.

❖ 1. Take an Early Sample.

Teachers ask students to draw a picture of someone or something they know and care about. Students also label the picture and write an explanation. Children are asked to use their best spelling and writing skills.

Teachers assess students' work based on the "Developmental Stages of Writing— Individual Checklist" and the "Developmental Stages of Writing—My Class at a Glance" sheets (see Appendix). The writing samples are also used as a baseline for the portfolio. The developmental spelling level of each child is recorded on the class list, so the teacher can look at the class as a whole.

❖ 2. Check Students' Known Words.

Marie Clay, the founder of Reading Recovery and a noted reading and writing expert, refers to "known words" as those the student writes in standard spelling. At the beginning of the year, the teacher asks the class to write for a ten-minute period words they know how to write. After students run out of words, the teacher suggests prompts, with questions such as: "Can you write your name?" "Can you write names for people in your family—Mom? Dad?"

The teacher continues asking the children to write words she feels they know, such as *cat, like, love,* or other high-frequency words. At the end of ten minutes, the teacher collects her class's papers and files them. The lists can be analyzed for developmental spelling growth. Students who have scored the lowest are considered for the "Making Books" program (see Chapter 5).

❖ 3. Assess Letter Recognition.

If you have emergent readers and writers, you can assess students' letter recognition by asking them to write the upper- and lowercase letters you dictate. For example: "Write a capital *B.* Now, write a lowercase *b.*"

Later, ask your students to write the letter of the beginning sound of each word you dictate. Exaggerate the beginning sound when you say it. For example: "Write the first letter you hear in *ball.*" Record each child's performance by circling the known letters and sounds on the letter chart (see "Sound and Letter Recognition Record Sheet" in Appendix).

❖ 4. Dictate Sentences.

In grades one and two, you can check your students' sound knowledge by dictating two sentences. Look over what is expected at your particular grade level regarding spelling growth. Take some of your grade level's spelling words, and craft two sentences to dictate aloud.
• Score one point for each sound that is correct. Also note directionality, spacing, and punctuation.
• Place each dictation test in the appropriate place in the assessment binder, under the student's name.
• Circle "sounds known" on the letter-assessment sheet.

❖ 5. Analyze the Results.

Now create a "My Class at a Glance" sheet, and plan your focus lessons to meet your students' needs. For example, if you noticed you have five students who need help with directionality, meet with them in a flexible group to give them special support. Also, model directionality skills through Morning Message and through Shared Writing.

ONGOING ASSESSMENT

Ongoing writing assessment takes place through teacher observation and anecdotal comments, combined with portfolio observation and teacher/student writing conferences.

Often, students demonstrate what they are ready to learn by using the tool incorrectly. For example, Alex showed that he is ready to learn paragraphing, because he has incorrectly used the sign for paragraphs in his writing journal. The teacher continually designs lessons to meet students' needs and teaches new strategies in one-on-one conferences or in small-group or whole-class lessons.

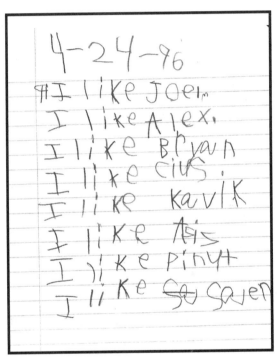

Alex is ready to learn about paragraphs.

USING CRITERIA CHARTS

❖ Benefits.

It's important to develop with students criteria charts on effective writing. This is crucial to students' understanding of what is expected of them during writers' workshop.

As teachers model during lessons, they add new skills—one at a time—to the writing-criteria chart.

It's also helpful to post criteria charts that can be used by students as a guide throughout the year. A typical kindergarten chart includes the following:

Our writing criteria—Kindergarten

1. The story make sense.
2. I leave spaces between words.
3. I use a period to tell something.
4. I use a question mark to ask a question.
5. I use an exclamation point to show I'm excited!

Melissa Miller's writing-criteria chart is creative, because she color coded the chart according to what was learned each grading period.

For example, the first grading-period criteria chart entries were in red, the second grading-period entries in blue, the third in green, and the fourth in purple. Students see-at-a-glance during which quarter they learned to add details to their writing. Color-coding is a helpful assessment tool for a teacher to quickly note at what time of year students have learned a writing skill. (Appendix contains the actual chart from her classroom, but it appears in black-and-white.)

❖ Developing Criteria Charts—Compare Two Models.

An easy way to introduce criteria charts is to show students a well-written writing sample and compare it with a poorly written sample. The samples should resemble your writers' varying abilities, but should be written by you.

Here are two actual examples, which were used in a first-grade class.

My Pet
 I have a pet dog. She is soft and yello. She has fur. I love her vry, vry much. She chazes me, but she is only playing. My dogs name is Rusty. She is fun.

SAMPLE 1

M Pt
 I hf a cat. Hiz nm is Bootz. He is nis.

SAMPLE 2

First-grade students noticed that both samples make sense. So they added "Make sense" to the criteria chart. They also included "Put details in your writing" and "Write a period at the end of a telling sentence." Children and teachers add to the chart all year.

Jane and Colin read over their kindergarten writing chart.

TYPES OF WRITING ASSESSMENT LOGS

❖ Learning Logs and Reading Logs.

The purpose of assessment is to gather data about children's writing progress and to design whole-class, small-group, and individual lessons which meet children's needs.

Learning logs and reading logs give the teacher information about students' progress. They also provide her with responses to what children learned from lessons in the content areas and from reading children's literature. In addition, the teacher assesses each student's writing progress by looking at the gradual differences in the dated entries (see Chapter 6).

PORTFOLIO ASSESSMENT

For the past seven years, our kindergarten-through-grade-six staff has been using portfolio assessment as an alternative assessment tool. *(Portfolios in the Classroom: A Teacher's Sourcebook* is the resource co-authored by Mary Dill, Nancy Areglado, et al.)

Writing is a natural component in a portfolio program. Our students routinely choose writing samples for their portfolios. These samples are selected from students' journals or writing folders. Writing is also connected to Rolling Valley portfolios as students choose learning-log or reading-log entries. Our school-based research has shown that portfolios raise children's self-esteem, motivate students to achieve their portfolio goals, and help them to be more connected to their learning. For each

Brett decorates the fourth-quarter folder for his portfolio.

piece that students choose for the portfolio in all grades, beginning with grade one, students self-evaluate what they have done well and set goals for future progress.

Students attach their evaluations and goals to each entry. Usually, one entry is chosen for each component. For example, in the writing area, students choose one piece from their learning log, one piece from their reading log, and one piece of writing from their journals or writing folders. Evaluations are done on unedited pieces. For example, all the steps of the writing process may be included in the portfolio, but the part that is evaluated by children is the unedited draft.

❖ Baseline Samples.

Baseline samples are students' first portfolio pieces. They are a student's earliest samples of work representing each of the components you select, for example, reading-journal entries, learning-log entries, and first pieces of writing. The first audiotapes and videotapes students make can also serve as baseline samples.

Baseline samples, collected during the first week of school, are compared to others collected throughout the year to assess growth and achievement. These samples are also useful in tailoring lessons to meet the needs of your children.

Kelsey is comparing her baseline samples to other samples in her portfolio.

❖ Students Choose Portfolio Samples.

All other samples in the portfolio are chosen by students, with one exception. If a child's choice shows work that is not as well-done as current performance indicates, the teacher has the option of also selecting a sample of the student's work. However, the child would still attach a self-evaluation and a goal to this sample. The teacher's comment is a generic one, because the sample has been taken so early in the school year that the teacher hasn't taught focus lessons yet. She is just assessing where students are at this point in the year, so it is not necessary to write narrative comments. All comments are written directly to the child. The following are samples of generic comments:

• Writing Sample:
"This is your baseline writing sample. Please notice if your writing made sense and stayed on-topic. This sample will be compared to others you write this year in your portfolio."

• Learning Log:
"This is your baseline learning-log sample. It shows what you learned in math, science, social studies, or health. All other samples in your learning log will be compared to this sample."

• Reading Log:
"This is your baseline reading-log sample. It shows what you learned about the book you read. All other samples in your reading log will be compared to this sample."

❖ Portfolio Guidelines.

For all samples in the portfolio, teachers write comments that state what the child did well on that item. Comments are addressed directly to the student and are completed after the portfolio self-evaluation and goals have been written by the student. Sometimes, the teacher comments on how the student's goal matches the selected piece.

At Rolling Valley, key threads are woven through the portfolio program. All portfolios are used as supplements to the report cards, and are shared in conjunction with the report cards. Parents routinely tell us, "The report card tells us the grade, but the portfolio explains the reasons for the grade. It lets me see how my child is doing and what my child is learning."

The concept of portfolios is explained to students early in the year, when baseline samples are collected. Students understand that the portfolio will show their parents some of the wonderful things children do in school. Then, throughout the grading period, criteria charts for each component are developed interactively with the students.

All portfolio samples have:
• a self-evaluation of what the child thinks he/she did well in that sample;
• a goal for that sample for the next grading period.

In addition, each piece (with the exception of kindergarten) contains a teacher comment. Teachers comment on areas in which the student did well in that piece. Often, the teacher mentions how appropriate the child's goal is. For each portfolio component that is selected, such as the learning log, students choose one "best piece."

Students, rather than teachers, choose samples for their portfolios. Exception? When the teacher finds that the child's selection does not reflect best work.

❖ Self-Evaluation.

We teach children how to self-evaluate their pieces. We begin by placing children in cooperative groups, and model how to evaluate a student writing sample. With a criteria chart posted, children write an evaluation of the piece. We ask the children to share strengths of the piece.

Then children are ready to select their own piece of writing to evaluate. We encourage children to refer to the criteria chart and evaluate the strengths of the piece they wrote. In particular, we ask them to comment on: "What did you do well?"

❖ Teaching Goal Setting.

Once children are familiar with self-evaluation, we introduce goal setting. In self-evaluation, children look for strengths in their writing samples. In goal setting, children identify areas for improvement.

We introduce the concept of a goal.

A goal is:
- **clear**—It's easy to understand.
- **specific**—It gives details and exact amounts, and stipulates how the goal will be accomplished.
- **realistic**—It's one that the student can really achieve.
- **challenging**—It's not too hard, not too easy, but just right.

❖ Helping Children With Their Goals.

Students practice looking at a mock sample of writing, pretending it is their own, and pointing out the things the writer did well. They also point to the criteria chart as evidence.

Students also look at the same piece and find a goal to improve it. For example, the student may write: "My writing shows I can make sense and use a period to tell things. My goal is I will add details to my writing. I will accomplish this goal by proofreading my reading and placing a caret wherever a detail needs to be added."

If the student wrote, "I will add details to my writing," the teacher notices a problem. She'll say, "Your goal matches your writing. Good job! How will you accomplish your goal?" Then, the teacher asks the student to add to the goal and tell how it will be accomplished:

Sandra: My goal is to use punctuation in my writing.
Teacher: That's an interesting goal. What type of punctuation are you referring to?
Sandra: I want to learn to use marks when people are talking.
Teacher: That's specific, Sandra. What do you call those marks?
Sandra: I used to call them talking marks, but I know there's another name.
Teacher: Right! We call them quotation marks. How can we add more details to your goal—to make it clearer for the reader and for you?
Sandra: Next quarter, I want to use quotation marks.
Teacher: How will you accomplish that goal?
Sandra: I'll read over my writing and make characters do some talking by adding quotation marks.
Teacher: That sounds like an excellent goal, Sandra. Can you add the part about using quotation marks to your goal? Can you also tell what you just said about how you will accomplish it?
Sandra: Sure!

KINDERGARTEN

❖ Baseline Samples and Beyond.

At the beginning of the year, Mrs. Godwin introduces the concept of a portfolio by sharing an actual artist's portfolio with the children. The children can relate to the artwork and understand it is a special collection of work.

Mrs. Godwin tells students that just as artists place their best pieces in their portfolios, students will do the same thing. Children will choose their best pieces of work over the year, to show their parents how well they're doing in school.

Of course, Mrs. Godwin also introduces parents to portfolios at Back-to-School Night. In addition to providing a rationale for portfolios, she also gives parents a brief overview of the portfolio process, and the portfolio components. Mrs. Godwin also meets with each child's parents and shares the report card and portfolio at the fall parent/teacher conference. Parent conferences provide an excellent setting to individually review all aspects of the portfolio process.

❖ First-Quarter Baseline Samples.

In kindergarten, the first-quarter samples are baseline only (not self-evaluated), because five-year-olds are so new to school.

What samples are placed in the portfolio?
Collected in a small-group setting:
• journal entry
• learning log
• self-portrait
• directed art sample (Example: "Make a school bus whose corners are round and wheels are cut from squares.")

Collected individually:
• interview

At the parent conference, held at the end of the first quarter, Mrs. Godwin shares the contents of the portfolio with the parents. She explains that the portfolio will be sent home each quarter, accompanied by a letter describing its contents, and by the child's report card. Mrs. Godwin also asks that the portfolio be returned to school with all its contents. Parents view the portfolio as an excellent way for their child to see growth in writing throughout the year.

❖ Second Quarter.

To the portfolio, Mrs. Godwin adds four new components. These include:
• writing to accompany the self-portrait (what students would like to tell about themselves)

• student evaluation of their writing (called the "I can ____" paper)

• writing to accompany the directed art (explains how the project was completed)

• teacher note to the student about progress visible in the portfolio

❖ **Third and Fourth Quarters.**
Portfolio elements include:

• journal writing

• learning log

• self-portrait with writing

• directed art with writing

• student evaluation

• interview

• teacher's note (third quarter) and comprehensive comments (fourth quarter)

Scott has told how he made the fourth-quarter directed art sample of a crocodile. He mentions several of the steps he followed.

Scott made a self-portrait and wrote a description of his picture. He told about how he looks at the sun.

Mrs. Godwin has written a comprehensive comment to evaluate Scott's portfolio components for the fourth quarter. She focuses on the positive and has addressed her comments to Scott.

Kindergarten self-portrait sample and student's comments assess art growth.

At the end of the fourth quarter, Mrs. Godwin confers with each of her students and reviews the contents of their portfolios. Together they talk about the progress the child has made, and the child dictates to the teacher what he or she can do.

The teacher uses this written prompt: "When I look at my portfolio, I see that I can _____." This is a valuable experience for the child to see how he or she has progressed throughout the year.

At the bottom of the form is a statement entitled "My goal is _____." Mrs. Godwin conducts a total-class lesson for goal setting. After presenting the goal-setting lesson, Mrs. Godwin conducts the individual end-of-the-year conference and sets a writing goal with each child. Goal setting is *only* done at this time.

Name: Scott

When I look at my portfolio I see that I can: Write words and leave spaces.

My goal is: To write more words.

Scott has shown he has made great progress in his portfolio this year!

Mrs. Godwin holds an end-of the-year conference with Amber.

FIRST GRADE

❖ Self-Evaluation.

"A helpful tool that made the self-evaluation process easier for my students was a yellow highlighter. My students used this to highlight the areas of a selection that shows what they did well. I showed my children that they could use the highlighted paper as a guide for filling out the 'I Can _____' sheet. They simply look at their writing, note what they did well, then fill in the 'I Can _____' sheet." —Lisa Holm

❖ Portfolios.

First-grade teachers include these components in the portfolio:
• list of books read
• writing sample
• reading-log sample
• an interview
• audiotape of a book that the child read aloud

The pieces of Lisa Holm's first-grade portfolio that are included show an example of a

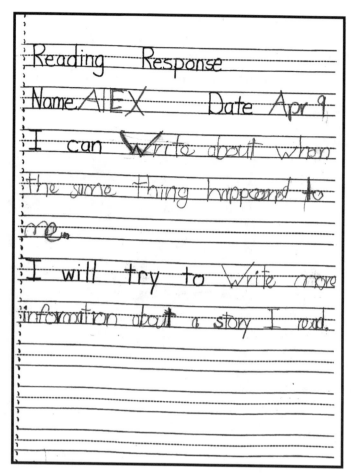

Reading Response

Name ALEX   Date Apr 9

I can Write about when
the same Thing happend to
me.

I will try to Write more
informaton about a story I read.

A first-grade reading-journal sample—with student self-evaluation, goal, and teacher comment—shows how helpful a portfolio can be.

reading-journal response, a writing sample, and a conference sheet. The student's self-evaluation and goal are attached to the reading-journal and writing samples. Lisa's comment is written on an index card and also is attached to the portfolio entry.

In the sample below, Alex has evaluated his reading-journal entry. Lisa Holm has written her comment on the original piece that Alex tore from his reading journal. Students always place the original pieces in the portfolio. If they tear an entry from a log, they write on the tab remaining on the ripped page where the sample went. For example, "Portfolio Reading-Log Sample—first quarter."

In the sample on the following page, Alex has included all of the steps of the writing process. He also self-evaluated and set goals for his writing. Lisa Holm commented on what he did well in his writing.

Lisa Holm also used the portfolio as part of Student-Led Portfolio Conferences, which she conducts during the second and third grading periods.

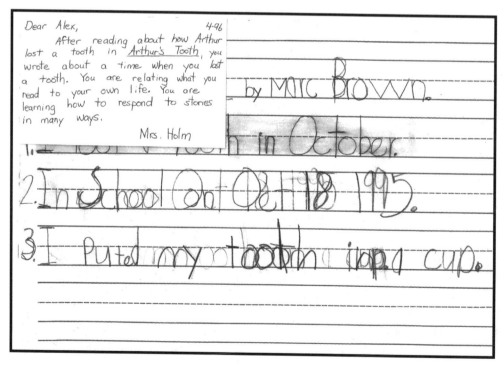

Dear Alex,   4-96
    After reading about how Arthur
lost a tooth in _Arthur's Tooth_, you
wrote about a time when you lost
a tooth. You are relating what you
read to your own life. You are
learning how to respond to stories
in many ways.
                        Mrs. Holm

by MArc BroWn.

1. I lost a Tooth in October.

2. In School On Oct-18 1995.

3. I Puted my tooth in a cup.

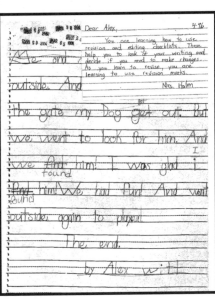

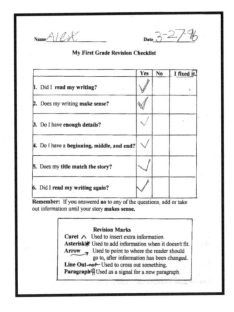

First-grade writing sample with student self-evaluation, goal, and teacher comment.

Chrysantemum
By Kevin HenKe
Why did The
author
Write the BOOK?
So peply was not
Call amr peply
names

READING JOURNALS

Reading journal entries are your responses to books you have read or heard read aloud. Responding in your reading log in different ways helps you to think more carefully about what was read. Your sample is the baseline, which will be used for comparison in showing how you grew in your understanding of literature.

Kelsey's baseline reading log response and teacher's generic comment.

SECOND GRADE

❖ Portfolios Benefit Everyone!

"I've found that reviewing portfolios and conferring with children as they examine their portfolios are my greatest assessment tools. All the information I need is in one place. The students get as many benefits as the teacher.

"One of the best parts of student self-evaluation is that the students write each of their portfolio goals on a goal sheet, which is laminated and taped to their desks each quarter. Therefore, it is easy for both the student and the teacher to think about goals.

"I take notes on the students' goals and plan my focus lessons to help students achieve their goals. For example, if a student writes, 'I want to add more details in my writing. I will accomplish this by proofreading my work and using carets to add details,' I plan lessons that address those skills."

—Melissa Miller

Name Kelsey   Date 10,25,95

First Quarter
Writing Sample Evaluation

This is what I did well:
I used my best handwriting. I
Put Perieds. I only get one wrd
rang.

These are my goals:
I will Put Periods I will Use
Smaller spaces.

Teacher comments:
Kelsey,
You have been doing a very good
job with details. You have great
ideas! I'm glad you were able to
see that you can work on using
periods correctly. Good job!

Kelsey 10,23,1995
There's A Monster In My
Drawer.
One day Abby get up
and get drasy wan she
opne hre grow she sav
samthing move. a fow week
ago, she last hre mavs.
Abby wandrd. "na it knt be
she sad. the samthing hpnd
but wan she pld out hre

favrat shrt it had olar
in it do you thenk
it was the mavs or a
monster?

Kelsey,
What a great story!
You used details
and original ideas.
Good job! Keep
working on periods and
proofreading.

Kelsey's first-quarter writing sample, self-evaluation, goal, and teacher comment show how well she writes.

Name __Kelsey!__ Date __10-26-95__

First Quarter
Reading Log Evaluation

This is what I did well:

I Put my name and data.
I Put some details
I Put the title. I Put
Periods, I use Pratd good
hand writing

These are my goals:

I will wit (write) more about
the book and wat (what) the
did.

Teacher comments:
Kelsey,
You did a great job of evaluating
your work. I like the way that
you chose an appropriate goal and
put it into your own words. Good job! ☺

Kelsey 10-9-95

The Ghost Eye Tree
By Bill Martin jr
Retelling

I thek The boy was
Sard of The Ghost Eye Tree
The girl was sordv Sard.
Wan they came back I thek
they wr the sardis do you?
and naw hes navr a rawd wan
Mommy wants Milk.

Kelsey,
You told your
feelings about the
book. Remember, a
retelling tells what
happened in the
book - not your
feelings. ☺

Kelsey's first-quarter reading-log sample, self-evaluation, goal, and teacher comment show what she knows about literature.

Name __Kelsey__ Date __Nov. 3 1995__

First Quarter
Learning Log Evaluation

This is what I did well:

I copy dawn the question
and ansd it. I drw a Picshr
and mowst of wit I lrn

These are my goals:

I will use mowr facts
I will be mowr (more)
Specific.

Teacher comments:
Kelsey,
You did a good job of
evaluating your work. You chose
a good goal that will help
you to improve your learning.
log entries. ☺

Kelsey 11-2-95

The Village of Round and Square House

① How is the Village
like VA?
all of the pepel
wam close they all
have names they all
eat and Play and swam
② How is it different
form VA?
it has volcanos
and square and Round
House The House
are mad out of strou
it has a Lit of onpin
Land

Good comparisons!

Kelsey's first-quarter learning-log sample, self-evaluation, goal, and teacher comment show what she has learned.

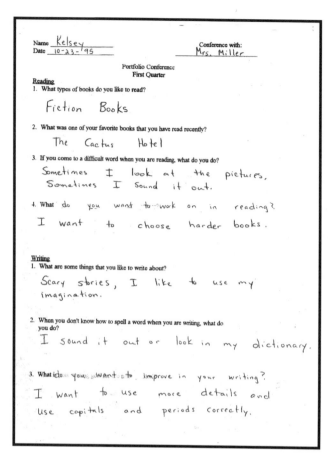

Kelsey's first-quarter portfolio conference sheet illustrates her thoughts about reading, writing, and goals for the next quarter.

❖ **Portfolio Conferences.**

Typically, we hold conferences toward the latter part of a quarter. At Rolling Valley, we have used four types of conferences.

• **Type One:**

Teacher/Student Portfolio Conference

Notice the sample of the conference sheet in Kelsey's grade two portfolio. Mrs. Miller conducted the conference with Kelsey about her portfolio. It includes questions about writing and reading. Mrs. Miller recorded what Kelsey said. Students are given the questions ahead of time, so children can think what their responses will be.

In the past, teacher/student portfolio conferences were held at the end of the first, second, and third grading periods. But it proved impossible for all of our teachers to confer with every student in the class-room, so Nancy Areglado trained volunteers to conduct conferences.

• **Type Two:**

Volunteer/Student Conference

In this type of conference, administrators and specialists help classroom teachers conduct portfolio conferences. Parents also assist.

The volunteer does a number of things:
• welcomes the student at the conference by noting something positive that is immediately visible in the child's portfolio;
• listens as the child shows and explains the portfolio components;
• checks student's goals to make sure they are clear, specific, realistic, and challenging;
• asks the questions requested by the teacher and records student's responses.

Volunteers end the conference on a positive note. Although these have been highly successful, some students have commented that meeting with their parent is more special.

• **Type Three:**

Student-Led Portfolio Conference

In student-led conferences, the student meets with their parent and explains to Mom or Dad the portfolio. The student also answers questions about how the portfolio shows improvement. The teacher takes a facilitative role. These conferences are held at the end of the second and third quarters.

• **Type Four:**
Peer Portfolio Conferences—Portfolio Partners
During the last grading period, students confer with students. A lesson conducted by the teacher prepares the children for how to confer with a friend. Teachers select the partners, based on which students work well together. Then, after grouping the children, the teacher shows a practice sample on the overhead projector for partners to evaluate. The partner comments only on what the writer has done well.

Partners role-play how to sit side-by-side, so each can see the other's piece of writing. Partners also practice how to look at the other person's writing sample while the author reads the piece aloud. After practicing in partner groups, the children actually evaluate each other's work.

All of these responses are labeled as being written by the portfolio partner, and they are attached to the portfolio sample. Students are encouraged to respond in sentences. For example, "My partner's writing showed he made sense." Portfolio-partner conferences are used in grade one and higher.

Portfolio-partner comments can take the place of teacher narrative comments, and they also take the place of any other type of conference during the last grading period. During the last quarter, students reflect on their portfolio progress, sharing their thoughts by sending the teacher a note telling how they achieved their goals and how the portfolios show growth during the school year.

Chapter Eight

Involving Parents *in the* Writing Program

*I*t is late August. This year, I think to myself, I will work even harder to strengthen the bond between home and school. This year will be my best year yet in communicating with my students' parents! How many times have you whispered those resolutions, only to be disappointed when just three parents—rather than thirty—show up for your first parent program?

What is the secret to successfully involving parents? Consistency and persistence. These two qualities build trust. If we begin a monthly newsletter in September, we need to continue to send it home consistently, all year long. Persistence is crucial because not all parents will be enthused about our efforts to involve them. So if one idea for involvement doesn't work, we haven't failed! We simply try another.

Ideas *for* Strengthening Parent Involvement

PUBLISH A MONTHLY NEWSLETTER

Parents enjoy receiving news from you and from your class about what their child is learning.

Here are some suggestions of what you might share with parents:
• an overview of the skills that the students are learning
• relevant information about how parents can become involved with the upcoming themes and events for the current month. For example, you can keep parents informed of field trips, cultural events and activities to be held at school, as well as special programs and materials you might need. For example, if you've decided to make one of your centers literacy-based on a grocery store/restaurant theme, you might use the newsletter to ask parents to send in empty cereal boxes, cookie mix

Colin works in the computer lab publishing an article for the newsletter.

P.J. displays his copy of his class's newsletter.

boxes, tortilla packages, restaurant menus, and so forth.
• a description of the author you are studying that month, so that parents can visit the public library or bookstore to pick up the authors' books
• news about how parent support of the Book Club helps build the classroom library

Here are some ideas of what students can contribute:
• a news report about what they finished studying during the preceding month
• a news forecast from the students' point of view about exciting things that will be happening during the upcoming month
• published writing samples done by student authors
• news about memorable projects they've done. For example, students at Rolling Valley made blueberry muffins

after reading Robert McCloskey's *Blueberries for Sal,* as part of The Book n' Cook program, an idea created by a West Stockbridge, Massachusetts, teacher, Norma Comstock.

• news about which four students will be the "Student of the Week" for the upcoming month

• illustrations to accompany a newsletter article

• book reviews

Elizabeth designed the cover for her class's Fluffy the Cat newsletter. Students love to be involved in choosing a title for the newsletter and also designing the cover page.

TEACHER TIP

Send Your Writing Program Home

"Back-to-School Night is a great time to inform parents about your writing program. Explain the steps of the writing process as well as an outline of anticipated writing activities for the year. Supply parents with handouts about your program for them to read at their leisure. Share with them whatever they need to know to understand your approach to teaching writing—the developmental stages of writing, the role of temporary spelling, and how skills are taught in context through Morning Message. Always present your program with enthusiasm, and remember you can never communicate too much about children's progress and accomplishments.

Send home samples of children's work at each stage of the writing process—planning, drafting, checklist for revision, editing, and final copies—one set per quarter. Parents really "get it" when they have these examples to look at. Invite parents to write comments about finished pieces and to return them to school. Reading the parent comments can be insightful for both the student and the teacher. Also, assigning several writing projects to do at home actively involves the parents in the writing process."

—Melissa Miller

PLAN A COME-VISIT-MY-CLASSROOM DAY

Invite your students' parents to visit your class during school time to actually see the children using the elements of a readers' and writers' workshop. Encourage parents to participate in the process by your planning a Morning Message they can read aloud and complete with their child. For example:

Dear Parents,
We are very excited you are here t _ _ _ _! We will show you how we begin our day with a Morning Message. You'll get to write to us in our writing j _ _ _ _ _ _, and then we'll show you the way we can write stories. We'll finish by sh_ _ _ _ _ you how we can read.

Love,
The Kids in Grade One-A

HOST A YOUNG AUTHOR'S DAY CELEBRATION

You have been diligently working with your students during writers' workshop and their first pieces of writing are ready to be published. Why not involve parents in the publishing celebration? Prepare for it by taking a few pictures to be made into slides of your students as they work writing a web, drafting, revising, editing, and illustrating their final copies. Think about ways to transform your classroom into a literary tea room—white paper tablecloths, fresh flowers, and so forth.

Here is the agenda for the first Young Authors' Day Celebration:

• Each student greets his or her parents.
• Serve the refreshments next. (Yes, refreshments! Why? Some parents always seem to arrive late. This way they won't miss the main part of the program.)
• Show the slides. The children love watching them.
• Present the published book to each student. (The audience applauds as each child receives his or her book.)
• Children read their published books to their parents or to a volunteer who takes the parent's place. With older students who are writing longer stories, you might decide ahead of time to have them select a three-minute excerpt to read aloud.
• The students take their published book home, then can place it in the Reading Center in the classroom for others to read, if they wish.

Young Authors' Day can be held several times a year. It is an exciting and uplifting way for students to share their writing accomplishments with their parents.

SPONSOR A SATURDAY FAMILY FIELD TRIP

Plan a class field trip on a Saturday morning that reflects a theme that you have been studying in your class. Students' parents provide their own transportation for their family and meet you at the site. All siblings and other relatives are invited.

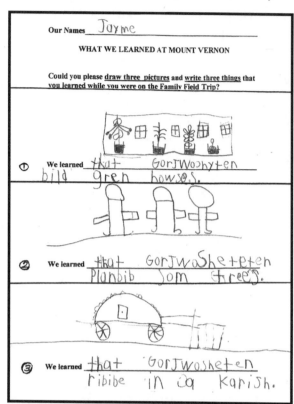

Jayme wrote and illustrated what she and her family learned on the Family Field Trip.

Visit the site ahead of time and plan activities for parents and children that involve writing and reading. Nancy Areglado organized a trip in Lisa Holm's first-grade class to Mount Vernon, George Washington's home, culminating the children's study of Washington. Nancy designed a Treasure Hunt Game for parents and students to play as they toured the beautiful grounds and mansion. Students used their reading skills as they located the trees labeled as being planted by George Washington. Nancy created a summary activity for students and parents that involved writing after they returned home from the trip. What was the parents response? "This was so much fun! Can we go on another one in the spring?"

DESIGN A FAMILY PROJECT CONNECTED TO A THEME

In Lisa Holm's first-grade class, Nancy Areglado taught a theme about plants. As a culminating activity involving parents and children, Nancy made planting packets for each student's family composed of a variety of seeds, soil, charcoal, as well as directions for planting seeds. She also designed a packet of plant experiments called "Having Fun with Plants." Students used writing skills as they kept a plant log at home of what happened in their experiments.

SHARE WITH PARENTS ARTICLES ABOUT WRITING

Share the research about writing development with parents, during Back-to-School Night, or Open House. Or during report card conferences, place a few articles on a table in the hall just outside of your classroom with a sign, "Please read this article while you are waiting for your conference." This gives parents a chance to become familiar with what is expected in young children's writing, and it helps them discuss their child's progress during the conference. In addition, share resources that have ideas for developing writing skills at home.

OUTFIT A WRITER'S BRIEFCASE

Stock an old briefcase or backpack with writing tools such as assorted markers, Color-Over markers, scented markers, colored pencils, crayons, scissors, glue, stapler, various sizes of colored construction paper for covers, half-picture, half-lined primary paper, lined primary paper, unlined paper, and blank books of various sizes. Attach a note that says:

Mary Dill encourages use of the Writers' Briefcase.

> Dear Author,
> Because you are a very special writer, you can take the Writers' Briefcase home. Choose whatever paper or blank book you'd like to write on. Bring what you write back to school to share in the Authors' Chair. If anyone in your family wants to write something to share, please also bring their writing to school. Please enclose a note from your Mom or Dad on the accompanying sheet. Have fun writing!
> Love,
Ms. Areglado

WRITERS' BRIEFCASE

Parents' Name _____

Child's Name _____

Our Family's Comments:

_____

_____

_____

_____

_____

USE A HONEY BEAR JOURNAL

Honey Bear is an adorable stuffed animal who needs a home. Consequently, Honey Bear goes to visit each child's home on a rotating basis. Honey Bear has a journal in the shape of a bear that is a log of what the bear does at each house. The parents and students write the log entry. It includes all the exciting activities that Honey Bear participates in with the family. Children really look forward to their weekend to have Honey Bear as a guest. Here is the note that is inside the cover of the Honey Bear journal.

Teacher volunteer, Kimberly Areglado, and P.J. discuss P.J.'s weekend plans for Honey Bear.

Dear Friend,
Thank you for letting me come and visit your house. If you want to read what other exciting things I have done at other friends' houses, just read my log. Please work with your mom and dad and keep a log telling what I did at your house when we celebrated my visit. Then, please bring me back to school on Monday, so I can continue my visits with other classmates. Thank you!
Love,
Honey Bear

Mary Dill feels the Home and School journal strengthens the home/school partnership.

LAUNCH A HOME AND SCHOOL JOURNAL

Bobbi Fisher, noted author and primary teacher, shared her idea of designing a Home and School Journal with Nancy Areglado. Nancy made 25 journals for her primary class in Massachusetts and labeled them, "Home and School Journal." Then, Nancy attached this note inside the front cover:

Dear Parents,
This is your special Home and School Journal for your child. Please write me notes in the journal containing your comments and questions about your child's writing and/or reading development, or whatever topic you'd like to discuss. For example, if you see your child writing at home, I'd love to know more about what your child wrote. Please

place this journal in your child's back pack and ask your child to give it to me. I will respond and send the journal back to you with your child on the same day I receive it.

Happy writing! I'll be looking forward to hearing from you.

Sincerely,

Nancy Areglado

TEACHER TIP

Parents Make Great Roving Editors

Parent volunteer, Kathy Reed, assists kindergarteners with their final copies.

During computer lab, I rely on parent volunteers to help me bring the children's revised writing to final copy. Parents assist the children when they type their work, either by helping read the editing and revision marks, or by inputting the text. Parents circulate throughout the lab assisting all students. The children really appreciate this extra support, and parents enjoy it because their role is well defined.

—Kathy Godwin

I like to play with Kristen.

Brook

Brook's final copy, completed in the computer lab.

TEACHER TIP

Ring Up a Writer at Home

"The winter of 1996 brought record snowfalls to our area. In fact, most of my students experienced the biggest snowstorms of their young lives. Needless to say, we had a lots of snow days. During one of these mother-nature inspired holidays, I made phone calls to my students. Without exception, each child was thrilled to receive my call! As we talked about the snow and the fun we were having, I suggested it might be fun to write about 'The Biggest Snowstorm Ever!' and then share our stories once we returned to school.

When classes resumed the following week, the children were eager to share. Over the course of the week, each writer took the author's chair and related his/her snow experiences. Because their writing sprung from what they knew, each child's work was authentic and had personal meaning.

While we may not have the inspiration of major snowstorms all through the year, we will have a host of other events and activities—each with the power to motivate writing. I believe that using personal phone calls at least once during the year will help trigger the home writing potential of my first graders."

—Lisa Holm

SOME CLOSING THOUGHTS

While home-school connections are a two-way street, you've got to be the one to encourage and inspire the relationship with parents. Keep them up to date, and keep them convinced that writing is meaningful and fun with writing adventures that involve who they are and what they do. And remember, if at first you don't succeed in involving parents in your writing program, try and try again!

Bibliography ⸺

CHILDREN'S BOOKS CITED

Altman, Suzanne. 1995. *My Worst Day Diary.* New York, NY: Bantam Doubleday Dell

Barrett, Judi. 1978. *Cloudy With a Chance of Meatballs.* New York, NY: MacMillan

Berger, Melvin and Berger, Gilda. 1994. *Where Does the Mail Go?* Nashville, Tennessee: Ideals Children's Books

Brett, Jan. 1990. *The Mitten.* New York, NY: Putnam Publishing Group

Brisson, Pat. 1992. *Kate on the Coast.* New York, NY: Macmillan Publishing Company

Brown, Marc. 1993. *Arthur's Tooth.* New York, NY: Little, Brown & Company

Brown, Margaret Wise. 1949. *The Important Book.* New York, NY: HarperCollins

Carle, Eric. 1994. *My Apron.* New York, NY: Putnam Publishing Group

Carle, Eric. 1993. *The Hole in the Dike.* New York, NY: Putnam Publishing Group

Celsi, Teresa. 1992. *The Fourth Little Pig.* Austin, TX: Steck-Vaughn Co.

Cherry, Lynn. 1994. *The Armadillo From Amarillo.* New York, NY: Harcourt Brace & Company

Christelow, Eileen. 1994. *The Great Pig Escape.* New York, NY: Clarion Books

Christelow, Eileen. 1995. *What Do Authors Do?* New York, NY: Houghton Mifflin Company

Clements, Gillian. 1988. *The Truth About Castles.* London, England: Macmillan Children's Books

Cooney, Barbara. 1994. *Only Opal—The Diary of a Young Girl.* New York, NY: The Putnam & Grosset Group

Cowley, Joy. 1990. *Joy Cowley Writes.* Bothell, WA: The Wright Group

Crews, Donald. 1991. *Big Mama's.* New York, NY: Greenwillow Books

Cummings, Pat. 1992. *Talking With Artists.* New York, NY: Bradbury Press

Dakos, Kalli. 1993. *Don't Read This Book, Whatever You Do!* New York, NY: Four Winds Press

Dakos, Kalli. 1990. *If You're Not Here, Please Raise Your Hand.* New York, NY: Four Winds Press

Dakos, Kalli. 1995. *Mrs. Cole on an Onion Roll.* New York, NY: Simon & Schuster Books For Young Readers

dePaola, Tomie. 1978. *The Popcorn Book.* New York, NY: Holiday

Dr. Seuss. 1958. *The Cat in the Hat Comes Back.* New York, NY: Beginner Books, Random House

Eye-Openers: *Insects and Crawly Creatures.* 1992. New York, NY: MacMillan Publishers

Gibbons, Gail. 1987. *Dinosaurs.* New York, NY: Holiday

Gibbons, Gail. 1982. *The Post Office Book—The Mail and How It Moves.* New York, NY: HarperCollins

Gibbons, Gail. 1983. *Sun up, Sun down.* New York, NY: Harcourt Brace & Company

Giff, Patricia Reilly. 1984. *Today Was a Terrible Day.* New York, NY: Puffin Books

Hantzia, Deborah. 1993. *Aladdin and the Magic Lamp.* New York, NY: Random House

Henkes, Kevin. 1991. *Chrysanthemum.* New York, NY: Greenwillow Books

Hopkins, Lee Bennett. 1993. *The Writing Bug.* Kaytonah, NY: Richard C. Owens Publishers

Hutchins, Pat. 1968. *Rosie's Walk.* New York, NY: Simon & Schuster

Hutchins, Pat. 1993. *The Wind Blew.* New York, NY: MacMillan

I Columbus—My Journal 1492-1493. 1990. Edited by Peter and Connie Roop. New York, NY: Avon Books

Johnson, Angela. 1989. *Tell Me a Story, Mama.* New York, NY: Bantam Doubleday Dell Publishing Group, Inc.

King, Virginia. 1990. *The Birthday Present.* Crystal Lake, IL: Rigby, a Division of Reed Publishing (USA) Inc.

Kraus, Robert. 1971. *Leo the Late Bloomer.* New York, NY: Simon & Schuster

Kroll, Steven. 1988. *Newspan Ned Meets the New Family.* New York, NY: Scholastic Inc.

Kruger, Carol. 1992. *The Spider and the King.* Crystal Lake, IL: Rigby Shortland Publications Limited

Joyce, Susan. 1994. *Post Card Passages.* Molalla, OR: Peel Productions

Leedy, Loreen. 1993. *Postcards From Pluto—A Tour of the Solar System.* New York, NY: Holiday House

Leedy, Loreen. 1990. *The Furry News—How to Make a Newspaper.* New York, NY: Holiday House

Martin, Bill. 1967. *Brown Bear, Brown Bear, What Do You See?* New York, NY: Henry Holt and Company

Martin, Bill. 1991. *Polar Bear, Polar Bear, What Do You Hear?* New York, NY: Henry Holt and Company

Meddaugh, Susan. 1992. *Martha Speaks.* New York, NY: Houghton Mifflin Company

McCloskey, Robert. 1944. *Make Way for Ducklings.* New York, NY: Penguin Company.

McKee, David. 1968. *Elmer.* New York, NY: Lothrop, Lee & Shepard Books

Mott, Winifred. 1990. *"It's Spring," Poetry Place Anthology.* New York, NY: Scholastic, Inc.

Pinkney, Andrea. 1994. *Dear Benjamin Banneker.* San Diego, CA: Gulliver Books

Rylant, Cynthia. *When I Was Young and in the Mountains.* New York, NY: Dutton, 1982

Smith, Judith and Parks, Brenda. 1984. *Jack and the Beanstalk.* Crystal Lake, IL: Rigby Publishers

Yashima, Taro. 1958. *The Umbrella.* New York, NY: Viking Press

Williams, Vera B. 1986. *Cherries and Cherry Pits.* New York, NY: William Morrow & Co.

PROFESSIONAL BOOKS ABOUT WRITING

Assessing—Primary Purposes Language Arts Guide. 1995. Fairfax, VA: County School Board, Fairfax County Public Schools

Avery, Carol. 1993. *...And with a Light Touch.* Portsmouth, New Hampshire: Heinemann Publishers

Clay, Marie. 1993. *Becoming Literate.* Portsmouth, NH: Heinemann Publishers

Calkins, Lucy McCormick. 1994. *The Art of Teaching Writing.* Portsmouth, NH: Heinemann Publishers

Clay, Marie M. 1993. *Reading Recovery—A Guidebook for Teachers in Training.* Portsmouth, New Hampshire: Heinemann Publishers

Clemmons, J., Laase, L., Cooper, D., Areglado, N., Dill, M. *Portfolios in the Classroom—A Teacher's Sourcebook.* New York, NY: Scholastic, Inc.

Dancing with the Pen—The Learner as a Writer. 1995. Wellington, New Zealand: Learning Media Limited

Depree, Helen and Iversen, Sandra. 1994. *Early Literacy in the Classroom.* Bothell, WA: Wright Group Publishing, Inc.

Dils, Tracey E. 1996. *Young Author's Guide.* Westerville, OH: Raspberry Publications

Fisher, Bobbi. 1991. *Joyful Learning.* Portsmouth, NH: Heinemann Publishers

Fletcher, Ralph. 1993. *What a Writer Needs.* Portsmouth, NH: Heinemann Publishers

Fraser, Jane and Skolnick, Donna. *On Their Way.* Portsmouth, NH: Heinemann Publishers

Gentry, J. Richard and Gillet, Jear Wallace. 1993. *Teaching Kids to Spell.* Portsmouth, NH: Heinemann Publishers

Graves, Donald. 1994. *A Fresh Look at Writing.* Portsmouth, NH: Heinemann Publishers

Graves, Donald. 1983. *Writing—Teachers and Children at Work.* Portsmouth, NH: Heinemann Publishers

Harwayne, Shelly. 1992. *Lasting Impressions.* Portsmouth, NH: Heinemann Publishers

Henderson, Kathy. 1993. *Market Guide for Young Writers—Where and How to Sell What You Write.* Cincinnati, OH: Writer's Digest Books

Hodgson, Mary. 1995. *Show Them How to Write.* Bothell, WA: The Wright Group

Lane, Barry. 1993. *After the End—Teaching and Learning Creative Revision.* Portsmouth, NH: Heinemann Publishers

Lyons, Carol A., Pinnell, Gay Su, and DeFord, Diane. 1993. *Partners in Learning.* New York, NY: Teachers College Press

Melton, David. 1985. *Written & Illustrated by....* Kansas City, Missouri: Landmark Editions, Inc.

Rico, Gabriele Lusser. 1983. *Writing the Natural Way.* Boston, MA: Houghton Mifflin Company

Writing—Primary Purposes, Language Arts Resource Guide. 1995. Fairfax, VA: County School Board. Fairfax County Public Schools

Children's Book List

BOOKS THAT INSPIRE STUDENTS TO WRITE

Alphabet Annie Announces An All-American Album by Susan Purviance and Marcia O'Shell (Houghton Mifflin, 1988). Students will have lots of fun listening to and reading these hilarious alphabet tongue twisters. Students may want to write their own alphabet book using similar alliterations—especially if you tell them that they can make up funny words to match the letter.

How a Book Is Made by Aliki (HarperCollins, 1986). This is a fascinating look at how a book is made, from the generation of the idea to the final, published copy on the library shelf. The animal characters and clear illustrations make the topic quite easy for students to comprehend. Your students will be more patient with the effort they put into writing after reading this book.

Where Does the Mail Go?: A Book about the Postal System by Melvin and Gilda Berger (Ideals Children's Books, 1994). If students want to know what happens to their letters after they are mailed, this children's book explains the answer. Students also learn about stamp collecting.

The Post Office Book: Mail and How It Moves by Gail Gibbons (Crowell, 1982). These books will motivate and intrigue students. They will want to write letters to their friends and family members. A fieldtrip to a local post office could be a great adventure. Letter writing is a natural spin-off.

BOOKS THAT FEATURE CHARACTERS WHO ARE WRITERS

Armadillo from Sasparillo by Lynne Cherry (Harcourt Brace, 1994). In this delightful tale, an armadillo named Sasparillo wonders how big the world is and where his place in the universe might be. So he travels from San Antonio, in the south of Texas, to Amarillo, a city in the north Texas Panhandle, sending postcards from each location he visits to his cousin, Brillo. This story is a good one for inspiring journal-writing or postcard-writing about a trip.

Communication by Aliki (Greenwillow, 1993). This book celebrates all aspects of communication. Diary writing, says the author, "Helps me understand what is troubling me... but my diary is for fun and news, too." Students quickly see how happy a note from a pen pal makes a friend who has moved away, and how great it is to receive a handmade birthday card. The colorful pictures throughout the book make it easily readable and very appealing to children.

Dear Benjamin Banneker by Andrea Davis Pinkney (Gulliver Books, 1994). Benjamin Banneker, the famous African American who worked to abolish slavery, used letter writing to truly great effect. Banneker's powerful letters to Thomas Jefferson persuaded Jefferson to see how wrong slavery was, and helped to change the course of history.

I Can Write by Rozanne Lanczak Williams (Creative Teaching Press, 1994).Rozanne wrote a book about all the surfaces she could write on and made it into a book that was published! Students should be encouraged to watch for reasons to write. Letters and notes to friends and relatives, a letter to get information, or party invitations. Many children love to fill out order coupons for free items. Sybil, Mary Dill's younger daughter, was famous for doing this! Mrs. Dill never knew what might come in the mail that Sybil had ordered. Sometimes the items were not free!

I, Columbus—My Journal 1492–1493 edited by Peter and Connie Roop (Avon Books, 1990). Students will be fascinated by the personal journal that Christopher Columbus kept during his trip to the New World. It's sure to encourage your students to write about their different adventures—even if they're not in the midst of discovering a new land!

Like Me and You by Raffi (Crown, 1994). This song shows how letter writing unites children from all over the world, conveying how every child is the same because each is "a child of a mother and a father, a very special son or daughter, a lot like me and you." This is a terrific song to use in conjunction with letter writing.

My Worst Days Diary by Suzanne Altman (Bantam, Doubleday, Dell, 1995). Mighty Mo knows the power of writing to help one keep an even keel. She writes in her Top Secret!! diary about her worst days. She discovers that the worst days can lead to the best. This is a good beginning chapter book, as it contains pictures.

Newsman Ned Meets the New Family by Steven Kroll (Scholastic, 1988). When Newsman Ned discovers that there is a new family in the neighborhood, he sharpens his interviewing skills as he attempts to locate the family so he can write a story about them. This is a humorous book that fits into a theme of family or a unit on the art of interviewing.

Only Opal , The Diary of a Young Girl by Barbara Cooney (Putnam, 1994). Opal Whiteley was born around the 1900s, and was adopted by a family from Oregon. They moved 19 times, from one lumber camp to another. Opal spent her days doing chores, such as churning butter, washing clothes, and carrying wood. But, being the curious child that she was, she would have rather been exploring the world around her. Each afternoon, Opal wrote about her life on any scrap of paper she could find. First published in 1929, this diary is a heart-warming account of about her life.

Kate on the Coast by Pat Bisson (Macmillan, 1992). Kate and her family were moving to the west coast from New Jersey. Like most children, Kate was a little uneasy about leaving all her friends and everything that was familiar. Kate found that as she wrote letters to her best friend back in New Jersey, there was a lot to do and see as they traveled from state to state. Her travel adventures included camping in Yosemite National Park, whale-watching off the Pacific coast, cheering for a dog-sled team, and exploring a Hawaiian island.

The Furry Newspaper by Loreen Leedy (Holiday House, 1990). Your young writers may just clamor to write and publish a class newspaper after reading this book. The animal characters make it all the more appealing for students to follow along as they gather information, write news and feature stories, and sell advertisements for their neighborhood paper, The Furry News.

BOOKS THAT SHOW HOW AUTHORS AND ILLUSTRATORS WORK

Chasing the Alphabet—The Story of Children's Author, Jerry Pallotta by Pamela Ryan (Shining Sea Press, 1993). This book will answer the many questions that children have about authors, and how they get their book ideas. Jerry grew up on Peggotty Beach in Scituate, Massachusetts, where he became knowledgeable about many different types of fish, such as goose fish, wolf fish, dogfish shark, and other marine creatures. He learned about the ocean by clamming, lobstering, and mossing (harvesting seaweed.) These childhood experiences inspired his first book, *The Ocean Alphabet Book*.

Talking with Artists by Pat Cummings (Bradbury, 1992). Fourteen favorite children's illustrators share their insights about where they get their ideas for what to illustrate, how they got started, and what is like to be an illustrator. The book is easy to read, and in addition to being an excellent resource for learning all about what illustrators do, it is also a model for how to conduct an interview.

What Do Authors Do? by Eileen Christelow (Houghton Mifflin, 1995). This is another book about how authors get their ideas and write their books. Eileen Christelow says "she focuses on authors in the context of their every day lives: The mundane events that can inspire stories at the most unexpected moments, with similarities between a child's struggle to write a story and an authors struggle to give birth to a book...."

The Writing Bug by Lee Bennett Hopkins (Richard C. Owns, 1993). This book is one of a series about authors, called *Meet the Author*. Students learn all about how Lee Bennett Hopkins became a writer, where he gets his ideas from, and what his studio looks like.

Appendix

ASSESSMENT FORMS

CRITERIA CHARTS FOR WRITING

STEPS OF THE WRITING WORKSHOP

REVISION AND EDITING CHECKLISTS

AUTHOR'S PLANNING PAGES

WRITING AWARDS

Developmental Stages of Writing Individual Checklist

Student's Name _____ Date _____

STAGE	EXAMPLE OF WRITING		
Scribbling			
Letter-like Symbols			
Strings of Letters			
Strings of Letters/ Some Beginning Sounds			
Consonants Representing Words			
Initial, Middle, and Final Sounds			
Transitional Phase			
Standard Spelling			
	Yes	**No**	**Not Applicable**
Makes Sense			
Writes in a sentence			
Story contains a beginning, middle, and end			
Contains details			
Shows evidence of revision			
Shows evidence of editing			

Developmental Stages
of Writing
My Class at a Glance

Date _____

Students' Names

	Scribbling	Letter-Like Symbols	Strings of Letters	Strings of Letters, Some Beginning Sounds	Consonants Representing Words	Initial, Middle, and Final Sounds	Transitional Phase	Standard Spelling

Let's Write

Sound and Letter Recognition Record Sheet

Directions: Circle all the letters and sounds the student knows.

Sounds Known

A B C D E F G H I J K L M N

O P Q R S T U V W X Y Z

Uppercase Letters Recognized

A B C D E F G H I J K L M N

O P Q R S T U V W X Y Z

Lowercase Letters Recognized

a b c d e f g h i j k l m n o

p q r s t u v w x y z

Name _____

Class Anecdotal Record Sheet

Topic Assessed _____

Date/Dates of Assessment _____

Adapted from Anecdotal Record Sheet
Fairfax County Public Schools

Let's Write

Things _____ Can Do

_____

_____

_____

_____

_____

_____

_____

_____

_____

_____

_____

_____

_____

_____

_____

Adapted from Donald Graves's work

Let's Write

Skills _____ is working on

Skill	Date Started	Date Completed

Adapted from Donald Graves's work

I Can Write About...

_____

Writing Completed by _____

Title	Genre	Date Started/Completed	

Adapted from Donald Graves's work

Let's Write

My Experiment Sheet

My Name: _____

Name of my experiment: _____

My Predictions: _____

_____

_____

My Observations:

My Conclusions and What I Learned:

_____

_____

_____

Teacher's Rating and Comments on the Process:

1 = Correctly completed task and explained concept; 2 = In the process of understanding the concept; 3 = No understanding of the process or the concept

Kindergarten Writing Criteria

1. I can draw a picture.

2. I can write letters.

3. I can write words.

4. I can leave spaces.

5. I can use stop signs (periods) to tell something.

6. I can use a question mark to ask a question.

7. I can capitalize the first letters in special names.

8. I can use an exclamation point to show that I am excited.

—By Mrs. Godwin's Class

Grade One Criteria Charts: Revision and Editing

What We Know About Revision:

- I can write about what I want to write.
- I can give a lot of information in my writing.
- I can write a story with a beginning, middle, and end.
- I can read what I have written to see if it makes sense.
- I can add details (little pieces of information) to make my writing more interesting.
- I can write facts.
- I can use a planning chart to help me write.
- I can use an asterisk * to add words in another place.
- I can use the Revision Checklist.
- I can use a caret mark ^ to add more words.
- I can use an arrow ➞ to show what to read next.
- I can make a line through (line-out) words I want to take out of my story.
- I can read to a friend what I have written.
- I can make changes after I read my story to a friend.
- I can write a title that goes with my story.

What We Know About Editing

- I can write my name.
- I can write the date.
- I can write a capital letter at the beginning of a sentence.
- I can use lowercase letters except for special names and the beginning of a sentence.
- I can put a period at the end of a telling sentence.
- I can put an exclamation mark at the end of an exciting sentence.
- I can put a question mark at the end of an asking sentence.
- I can leave two finger spaces between words.
- I can put a whole hand space at the beginning of a paragraph.
- I can use quotation marks " " to show when someone is talking.
- I can use the Editing Checklist.

—By Lisa Holms's Class

Grade Two Writing Criteria Chart

Second Grade Writers

1. Use details in your writing.
2. Write sentences that make sense.
3. Give each story a title.
4. Start sentences with a capital letter.
5. Use periods, question marks, and exclamation marks at the end of sentences.
6. Write your name and date.
7. Capitalize important places, names, and things.
8. Use your best handwriting.
9. Use your best spelling.
10. Look for mistakes and fix them.
11. Give your story a beginning, middle, and end.
12. Write sentences that sound right.
13. <u>Reread</u> your draft when you are done.
14. Use quotation marks when someone is talking.
15. Circle words you think are misspelled.
16. Use your dictionary or Franklin Speller to fix spelling.
17. Try not to start sentences with "and."

—By Mrs. Miller's Class

(This chart is color-coded by grading periods, so that students can see what was learned at different points in the year.)

Steps for Kindergarten Writing

- **Plan**
  ⟨ Brainstorm ideas
  ⟨ Color and label "I Can Write About"

- **Write** ~ Write your ideas.

- **Confer with Teacher**
  1. Read your writing to your teacher.
  2. Check "My Conference Checklist."

- **Place writing in the Publishing Tub.** Don't forget to include:
  1. finished piece
  2. conference sheet

- **Publish** ~ Illustrate your writing!

Our Steps for Writing — Grade One

- **<u>Plan</u>**   **Talk, Draw, Web**

- **<u>Draft</u>**   **Write your ideas.**

- **<u>Check</u>**   **Do the Revision Checklist.**

- **<u>Confer</u>**   **Read your writing to a classmate.**

- **<u>Revise</u>**   **Fix your draft.**

- **<u>Edit</u>**   **Do the Editing Checklist.**

- **<u>Publishing Box</u>** **Put your finished writing in the publishing box.**

- **<u>Confer with Teacher</u>**

- **<u>Publish</u>**   **Use the Publishing Center!**

Steps for the Writers' Workshop
Grade Two

1. Plan

2. Draft

3. Reread your draft two times.

4. Complete the Revision and Editing Checklists.

5. Write your name on the chalkboard to work with a buddy.

6. Revise and edit with a buddy.

7. Reread your draft that's been revised and edited.

8. Put it in the publishing tub.

9. Confer with the teacher.

10. Publish (rewrite or use the computer). Illustrate.

—Melissa Miller

Up and Down the Writing Staircase

Publish

Confer with a teacher

Confer with a buddy and edit

Edit own writing

Confer with a buddy and revise

Revise

Draft

Plan

My First Grade Revision Checklist

	Yes	No	I fixed it.
1. Did I **read my writing?**			
2. Does my writing **make sense?**			
3. Do I have **enough details?**			
4. Do I have a **beginning, middle, and end?**			
5. Does my **title match the story?**			
6. Did I **read my writing again?**			

Remember: If you answered **no** to any of the questions, add or take out information until your story **makes sense.**

Revision Marks

Caret	^	Used to insert extra information.
Asterisk	*	Used to add information that doesn't fit.
Arrow	↗	Used to point to where the reader should go, after information has been changed.
Line-Out	~~not~~	Used to cross out something.
Paragraph	¶	Used as a signal for a new paragraph.

Designed by Lisa Holm, Melissa Miller, and Nancy Areglado
Rolling Valley School, Springfield, Virginia

Buddy's Name _____   Date _____

Writer's Name _____

First Grade Buddy Revision Checklist

	Yes	No	I fixed it.
1. Did **my partner read** his or her writing to me, and did I follow along, too?			
2. Does the writing **make sense?**			
3. Does the writing have **enough details?**			
4. Does the writing have a **beginning, middle, and end?**			
5. Does the **title match the story?**			

Remember: If you answered **no** to any of the questions, work together with your partner to fix his or her writing.

	Revision Marks	
Caret	^	Used to insert extra information.
Asterisk	*	Used to add information that doesn't fit.
Arrow	➚	Used to point to where the reader should go, after information has been changed.
Line-Out	n̶o̶t̶	Used to cross out something.
Paragraph	¶	Used as a signal for a new paragraph.

Designed by Lisa Holm, Melissa Miller, and Nancy Areglado
Rolling Valley School, Springfield, Virginia

Let's Write

My First Grade Editing Checklist

	Yes	No	I fixed it.
1. Did I **read my writing** to check on my editing?			
2. Did I start each sentence with a **capital letter**?			
3. Did I end each sentence with a **period**, an **exclamation point**, or a **question mark**?			
4. Did I use my **Writing Dictionary** to check my spelling?			
5. Did I **circle** any words I think are misspelled?			

Remember: If you answered **no** to any of the questions, try your best to fix your mistakes.

Designed by Lisa Holm, Melissa Miller, and Nancy Areglado
Rolling Valley School, Springfield, Virginia

First Grade Buddy Editing Checklist

	Yes	No	I fixed it.
1. Did **my partner read** his or her writing to me, and **did I follow along**, too?			
2. Did my partner start each sentence with a **capital letter**?			
3. Did my partner end each sentence with a **period**, an **exclamation point**, or a **question mark**?			
4. Did my partner use his or her **Writing Dictionary** to check how words are spelled?			
5. Did my partner **circle** any words that he or she thought were misspelled?			

Remember: If you answered **no** to any of the questions, work together with your partner to fix his or her writing.

Designed by Lisa Holm, Melissa Miller, and Nancy Areglado
Rolling Valley School, Springfield, Virginia

Let's Write

My Second Grade Revision Checklist

	Yes	No	I fixed it.
1. Does my writing **make sense**?			
2. Does it **sound right**?			
3. Do I have enough **details**?			
4. Do I have a **beginning**, **middle**, and **end**?			
5. Does my **title** match the story?			

Remember: If you answered **no** to any of the questions, add or take out information until your story **makes sense**.

My Second Grade
Buddy Revision Checklist

	Yes	No	I fixed it.
1. Does my partner's writing **make sense**?			
2. Does it **sound right**?			
3. Does my partner have enough **details**?			
4. Does my partner have a **beginning**, **middle**, and **end**?			
5. Does my partner's **title** match the story?			

Remember: If your buddy answered **no** to any of the questions, work together to fix your writing.

Let's Write

My Second Grade Editing Checklist

	Yes	No	I fixed it.
1. Did I end each sentence with a **period**, an **exclamation point**, or a **question mark**?			
2. Did I start each sentence with a **capital letter**?			
3. Did I use **quotation marks** to show when someone is talking?			
4. Did I use my **dictionary** to check my spelling?			
5. Did I **circle** any words I think are misspelled?			

Remember: If you answered **no** to any of the questions, try your best to fix your mistakes.

Buddy's Name _____ **Date** _____

My Second Grade Buddy Editing Checklist

	Yes	No	I fixed it.
1. Did my partner end each sentence with a **period**, an **exclamation mark**, or a **question mark**?			
2. Did my partner start each sentence with a **capital letter**?			
3. Did my partner use **quotation marks** to show when someone is talking?			
4. Did my partner use my **dictionary** to check his or her spelling?			
5. Did my partner **circle** any words he or she thinks are misspelled?			

Remember: If your buddy answered **no** to any of the questions, work together to fix your mistakes.

Kindergarten Author's Planning Page

My Conference Checklist

☐ **Name**

☐ **Date Stamp**

☐ **Draft Stamp**

☐ **Book Color**

☐ **Paper Size**

☐ **Put in Publishing Tub**

Designed by Kathy Godwin

First Grade Author's Planning Page

My Name _____

Title of my Writing _____

Dedication _____

About the Author _____

_____

_____

_____

I want the color of my published book to be _____

I would like my published copy
- [ ] printed
- [ ] typed on the computer by me
- [ ] typed on the computer by me and a helper
- [ ] typed on the computer by a helper

I would like this kind of paper in my published book:
- [ ] paper with room for a picture by me
- [ ] paper with only words on a page

Certificate of Recognition for Writing

WRITER'S AWARD

is presented to

_____

for participation in the Writers' Club
for the ___ — ___ — ___ school year.

Certificate of Recognition

for Outstanding Writing

AUTHOR'S AWARD

is presented to

_____

for being published in

_____

for the ___ ___ ___ ___ school year